A DOG NAMED KING

THE TRUE STORY OF AN AMERICAN POLICE DOG

Commissioner Bratton,
All the best to
you & yours!

ANDREW C. REVERING

ISBN:
978-1-64184-407-9 (paperback)

Dedication

This book is dedicated to the memory of T. Patrick Cahill. From New York to San Francisco, he is known as "Mr. Cahill" to thousands who have benefited directly or indirectly from his pioneering efforts in police dog training. Mr. Cahill served fourteen years as a civilian head trainer for the Washington D.C. Metropolitan Police Department. While there, he had a profound effect on the development of American police dog work until his retirement in the early seventies. He originally served as a London Metropolitan Policeman in the 1940's and 1950's and was involved in the early development of police dog training across England and Europe. He came to the United States upon his retirement in 1958, to live with his daughter in Baltimore. Baltimore Police Department hired him to train their first police dogs that same year and in 1960 he was hired by Washington D.C. to train their dogs. I met Mr. Cahill in 1968, and we became good friends and fellow judges at National Police K-9 Trials. He was a mentor to all who knew him.

In recognition of the support, encouragement, and editorial work of Jennifer Kwasny and Stephanie Revering.

TABLE OF CONTENTS

PREFACE

Anoka, Minnesota Police Dog King was the first police dog to be used effectively in the Minneapolis/ St. Paul Metropolitan area in the 1960's. His success led to the development of police dog units in a five- state area surrounding Minnesota. He received numerous awards for criminal apprehensions, and a local newspaper reporter referred to him as the Rin Tin Tin of the Anoka Police Department. Upon his death the City of Anoka named a city park after him (King Memorial Park), and a bronze life size statue was placed there in his honor. In 2018 King was inducted as an honoree in the National Law Enforcement Museum in Washington D.C.

The story you are about to read is true, some names have been changed to protect the innocent.

CHAPTER 1
REX THE WONDER DOG

My first memories as a kid were living in Grove City, Minnesota, a city of about four hundred and fifty people at the time. My parents owned a gas station in which we lived on the second floor. My dad did mechanical and blacksmith work in the garage. I remember going to kindergarten in the Fire Hall. Our classroom was right next to the fire trucks. I thought that was really cool. My dad had a heart condition and his doctors told him for health reason he needed to get out of the blacksmithing and gas station business. As a result he purchased a beer tavern just outside of Litchfield, Minnesota. Growing up in Litchfield, Minnesota, I always remember having dogs in our family. My parents operated the beer tavern in the 1940's, 50's and early 60's. We lived in attached living quarters behind the tavern. The first dog I have a memory of was a black Labrador Retriever. My dad used him for hunting pheasant and duck His name was "Blacky" and to us he was just a regular member of the family. I had an older brother, Bob, a younger brother, Mick, and two younger sisters, Mary and Katie. We use to crawl all over Blacky and he would follow us and keep track of us wherever we went. My dad had passed away in his early 30's as a result of having Rheumatic fever as a kid, so Ole Blacky became even more important to all of us. He was that silent friend that was always there for hugs and comfort. When you looked into the sorrowful eyes of Ole Blacky, you knew he understood the loss being experienced of a caring father by very young children. I was eight years old when my dad passed.

When I was twelve years old I had a paper route to take care of. At that time, I had a German Shepherd/Collie mixed breed male dog

1

named Rex. Rex always went along with me on my paper route, when I rode my bike into town, as our beer tavern was about a mile and a half outside of the city. I also remember, there being a Mink Farm just on the edge of town, where I delivered papers. That Mink Farm had two big Alaskan huskie type dogs chained up on each side of a long driveway as you came up to the property. Both dogs were very aggressive and were intended to let strangers know that they weren't welcome. The owner quite obviously didn't want anyone stealing his very valuable mink. Rex always kept them distracted while I passed between them and delivered the paper to the front porch.

Andy Revering & Rex

I didn't have Ole Rex all that long when one day I was mopping the dance floor area of my Mom's tavern while she was in town grocery shopping. The tavern didn't open up until noon and it was a Saturday, and a part of my chores were helping to clean the place up from the night before. I heard what sounded like a pop coming from the back door area of the dance floor. At the same time I heard the pop, I heard what sounded like Rex yelping.

I went to the back door and as I started to open the door, I heard the pop again and Rex yelped. I now recognized the popping sound as a gunshot, and saw Rex on the back step bleeding. As I tried to coax him into the house, I heard the shot again and Rex yelped. At the same time I looked in the direction of the Litchfield Machine Shop which was directly across the parking lot from my mother's tavern. At the back door area of the machine shop which I knew to be the blacksmith section, I saw a man leaning out the sliding door with a rifle pointed in my direction. He fired the gun again and again at Rex as I tried to drag Rex into the house. My standing right next to the dog with my arm around him trying to coax him into the house didn't deter the shooter from continuing to fire. I don't remember ever having any fear of being struck by the gunshot as I was trying to drag Rex out of the line of fire, my only fear was that Rex might be killed. When I finally got Rex into the house I discovered he had been shot eight times; somehow, he survived. My mother arrived home shortly after all of this. She called the Sheriff's Department and helped me render first aid to Rex.

I learned later that the man who shot Rex was the blacksmith at the machine shop, and that he had been drinking heavily, and he didn't like Rex because he chased cars. That man was a regular patron of my Mom's Tavern, so we knew him personally.

After Rex was examined by the Vet we were told he had been shot with a 22 caliber rifle and that it appeared all of the rounds which struck him passed through without hitting any vital organs. I don't remember what the blacksmith was charged with; however, I do remember that he was terminated from his job. Rex survived his injuries. That alone, and the fact that he was my great protector on my paper route caused me to think of him as my wonder dog, but he continued to chase cars and was eventually struck by one and killed.

We continued to have dogs around during my grade school years, including my junior and senior high school experience, but none of them stood out to me like Ole Blacky and Rex.

I went to a one room country school house from 1st through 5th grades which was located about a mile and a half from my home.

The local Catholic Church had just built a new elementary Catholic School in Litchfield. My mother was of Italian descent and a serious Catholic, so she was determined to see all of us attend that school. The problem was that it only went up to 6th grade, which was the grade I would be attending. My older brother Bob was going to be a 7th grader. To make sure he didn't miss out on attending Catholic grade school, my mother sent him to live with our Grandparents in Urbank, Minnesota, which was about 150 miles North of Litchfield. Grandma Gertrude Ulman was my dad's mother.

While attending St. Phillip's School in the 6th grade, Sister Margaret Claire, who was the Principal and taught 6th grade, appointed me to be the Captain of the School Patrol. School Patrol Captains in elementary schools in Minnesota were invited to attend a week long summer camp at a place called Legionville in Brainerd, Minnesota. Legionville was sponsored by the American Legion and was a camp created specifically to teach school patrol captains how to provide safe street crossing for children. Minnesota State Troopers were the instructors. I was totally in awe of State Troopers as a 6th grader and I'm sure the experience led to my eventual career as a police officer. School Patrol Captains were supposed to take what they learned at Legionville and train the school patrolmen under them. I was the School Patrol Captain all three

years while at St. Phillips Elementary School, and never will forget the experience of Legionville.

In the winter of 1956, I was 13 years old and in 8th grade at St. Phillips School in Litchfield, Minnesota. I had a friend by the name of Jim, who was a foster child and lived with a farm family. Jim was a couple of years older than me, but was in the same grade in school. One Sunday that winter, Jim showed up at my place driving a brand new 1956 Oldsmobile two door hard top, sky blue and white. Jim wanted to know if I wanted to go skating in town. It wasn't unusual for Jim to be driving, as he was old enough to have a license, but I asked him, "Where did you get that car?" He said, "My uncle is visiting from Minneapolis and let me use it for a couple of hours." He said further, "It's a little low on gas, can you get a dollar from your mother?" My mother's beer tavern, by law, was not allowed to be open until Noon on Sunday's so she was napping on the couch. I woke her and said, "Jim is here and wants to go skating in town, but he is a little low on gas." She said, "Where did he get the car?" I said, "He told me his uncle is visiting from Minneapolis, and let him take it for a couple of hours." My mother knew Jim was a couple years older, had a license, and trusted him. She said, "Go ahead and take a dollar out of the till." Jim and I took off for Litchfield, and stopped at the first gas station on the West end. When the attendant came up he asked for a dollar's worth of gas. Just then, a police car

5

came by on Main Street and turned into the gas station. Jim put the Oldsmobile in gear and took off at a high rate of speed. The attendant at the gas station was barely able to pull out the hose from the pump. I asked Jim, "What is going on?" Jim said, "I stole this car." Turns out the police car that was chasing us was being driven by the police chief and he had the owner of the car with him. We hadn't gone very far when the car went into a skid on icy streets and slammed into a tree, and I went through the windshield. I remember waking up a couple of hours later in the hospital. I couldn't remember anything about what had happened. All I could remember was that I had to serve Mass that morning. I finally realized there was someone in the room lecturing me. It turned out to be the elderly Catholic Priest. My mother walked in about this time and said, "Andy did not know anything about this. Jim has already told the police what happened and you need to leave." He left. The lesson I learned from all of this, although many years later, when I became a local police officer, was to make sure I spoke to everyone involved in a stolen vehicle, as someone may be innocent.

Two guys that were my best friends in grade school were Neil Konietzko and Bob Olson. We had all decided we wanted to attend Nazareth Hall Seminary when we were in 9th grade to study for the Priesthood. The problem was that I didn't pass the entrance test, so those two guys went off to Nazareth Hall without me. My Uncle Carl Priley, who was my mother's brother, was a Catholic Priest. He told me, "Don't worry Andy, we're going to get you into Crosier Seminary at Onamia, Minnesota, which is in the Duluth Catholic Diocese, when you enter 10th grade."

Crosier Seminary, 1957.

At the end of my 10th grade in the Seminary, the good Crosier Fathers asked me not to come back. I was failing Latin and geometry and they thought I might be better suited for a different line of work. When my uncle, Father Carl Priley, learned of this, he said, "Don't worry Andy, you're going to have to do a year at Duluth Cathedral High School so that you can show the Bishop that you can cut it academically, then we'll get you back in the seminary." I started out 11th grade staying at St. James Catholic Orphanage in Duluth, where my mother and her siblings were raised after her mother died in 1918 of the Spanish Flu. I'd take a bus from the Orphanage downtown to Duluth Cathedral High School. At the end of the school day, I'd take a bus to the other end of town, as I was playing football for Cathedral, and they didn't have a football field near the school. Then, I'd take a bus all the way back to the Orphanage in the evening. I did that for three months before calling my mother. I told her, "Mom, I don't think this priest thing is going to work out. They've got the best looking Italian girls at this school that I've ever seen in my life." She said, "Your brother Bob will be up to pick you up in the morning." I returned to Litchfield, Minnesota, and finished out 11th grade at Washington High School.

Tom Mix Entertains Orphans

Tom Mix, premier cowboy of the screen, who is making a personal appearance at the Lyceum Theatre in Duluth, entertained 93 orphans at the St. James Orphanage yesterday. He is shown surrounded by his child audience. The young girl directly behind him and to his right is my mother, Eleanor Priley(Revering-Klindt). 1932.

CHAPTER 2

AIR FORCE SENTRY DOG

Two days after graduating from high school in Litchfield, I headed off to the United States Air Force. On June 6, 1961, I started Basic Training at Lackland Airforce Base in San Antonio, Texas. In the 1960's, there was still a draft in place, so my thought was that I might as well get this military service requirement out of the way before I got drafted. I had been approached by an Air Force recruiter during my senior year, so I had already signed up to leave for training right after graduation. I didn't think it was even unusual that I had not been approached by the Army, Navy, or Marine Corps recruiters. There was no war going on when I enlisted, so I presumed that recruitment was not being pushed all that much. I was only seventeen years old, and wouldn't be turning eighteen until December, so my mother had to sign a permission document for me to enlist. I knew that I didn't want to go to college at that time, and wasn't sure what I wanted to do with the rest of my life. So I thought I might figure it out while I was in the Air Force.

I traveled to San Antonio, Texas, by commercial airlines. It was the first time I had ever been on an airplane. I flew with Braniff Airlines, a popular airline of the 1960's. It was a four engine propeller driven plane. Jet planes were only beginning to become of age during this period, so there weren't many around yet. I had a window seat over the right wing. We hadn't been flying for more than an hour or so when I heard a sputter in one of the engines. I looked out the window and saw smoke, and fire began pouring out the front of one of the engines. The pilot came on the intercom and said they were having trouble with one engine. As he said that, I noticed the fire went out and the propeller on that engine stopped. The pilot came back on the intercom and said we would be landing in Tulsa, Oklahoma for repairs. The airline put us up in a hotel for the night while they repaired the engine, and the next day we flew out for Texas on

the same plane. This time everything went well. Basic training did not seem all that difficult, although I did have some minor problems performing some of the physical training. A Training Instructor detected it and sent me to see an Air Force Doctor. When he asked me about the large scars on my stomach area I had to tell him that I had ruptured a large intestine while playing football in high school, and surgery was performed to repair it in September of 1960. The Air Force Doctor told me I had major surgery only nine months ago and they could give me a medical discharge. I asked him, "If I could perform the physical training requirements would you let me stay in?" He said that it would be up to my Training Instructors.

I was determined to make it through the training. I didn't want to have a medical discharge on my records, which may prevent me from some future job that I might be interested in. I must have done okay, because my Training Instructors made me a Squad Leader and eventually the Dorm Chief, who was the enlisted trainee serving right under the Training Instructors. As the Dorm Chief, I had a hand in helping to lead my flight to earn "Honor Flight" during parade, which was a proud achievement for our unit. I never did tell the 50 guys I served with in the flight, and whom I was appointed to help supervise, that I was only seventeen years old and the youngest airman in our unit. I was told I always looked older for my age, and under these circumstances, I think that served to my advantage.

After basic training, an airman either received orders to attend specialized training, or was sent directly to an assigned Air Force Base for On the Job Training or OJT. My orders came through stating that I would report for OJT (on the job training) as an air policeman, and I was assigned to Blytheville Air Force Base in Blytheville, Arkansas. I was only seventeen years old and being assigned duties as an air policeman. That sounded exciting! My orders also said that I had fifteen days delay in route to my base, which meant I had fifteen days leave and could go home before reporting to my base. After the scary flight I experienced traveling to Texas, I didn't care if I ever flew again at that time, so I took a train all the way back to Minnesota. It took me two days with all the stops.

The leave time I spent back at my hometown in Minnesota seemed very short. I took a Greyhound Bus down to Blytheville Air Force Base. The City of Blytheville was a small community of 20,700 people and was located in the Northeast corner of Arkansas about 50 miles from Memphis, Tennessee. It was a very flat area and the city appeared to have large cotton fields on all sides. The Air Force base was located just about 2 miles outside of the city. Having grown up in central and mostly rural Minnesota, I had not had occasion to be around many African American people. In fact, I don't remember there being an African American family at all in my community. My first interaction with African Americans and Mexican Americans was during my basic training and I count them among the closest friends that I made during that experience.

Blytheville was different. The first thing I noticed when I got off the bus in the city was the "white only" signs as I went to use the bathroom at the bus stop. I wasn't even sure what those signs meant. When I learned what they did mean, my first reaction was that I thought we had settled this issue after the Civil War. Civil Rights Legislation had not been passed at this time, and it became clear to me in short order that segregation was still being practiced in the South in no uncertain terms. I learned a bit later that the city's African American population had an entirely separate area where they lived in this city, and that it was patrolled by the only two African American officers in the local police department. It was a disturbing issue for a seventeen year old white kid from central Minnesota, and an experience which I'll never forget.

Whites only sign

I caught a cab in front of the bus station and was dropped at the front gate of the Air Force Base. There was a huge sign next to the front gate which read Blytheville Air Force Base. It had an insignia with an iron fist holding lightning bolts and a scroll which read "Strategic Air Command". Underneath that it read, "Peace is our Profession". Being a rookie to the Air Force I didn't even know what Strategic Air Command, or SAC, meant. I would find out very soon.

The front gate to the base was manned by two very sharply dressed Air Policemen with white garrison caps, Black Sam Brown belts with holstered 45 caliber automatics, tan uniforms, and highly shined black combat boots with white laces. I was impressed, and pictured myself doing what they were doing.

I showed my orders to the Air Policemen at the front gate. One of them directed me to see First Sergeant Oller in the Orderly Room at the barracks of the 97th Combat Defense Squadron. First Sergeant Oller was a sort of portly, grey haired older man, who constantly had a lit cigar in his mouth. He was friendly enough, and kind of the fatherly type. He gave me some paperwork and sent me over to Base Supply to pick up all the proper Air Police uniform gear. When I got back, he assigned me to a room in the barracks with two other airmen. After living in a dormitory atmosphere in basic training I thought it was a lot more comfortable to be assigned to a room with two other airmen.

I learned that all the barracks on the base were made up the same way. Two to three airmen were assigned to a room and shared a latrine with two to three other airmen in an adjoining room. Sgt. Oller advised me that I was to join my two roommates in the morning and report for what he called guard mount. He said a Sergeant would be in charge of the guard mount and would assign me to a veteran Air Policeman with whom I would began my OJT. One of the Airman, who was in the room we share a latrine with was an African American, middle aged gentleman. His last name was Neely, and he was a Staff Sergeant. I came to like him and held him in high regard. He was always very friendly, and was highly respected as someone who had been around a long time and knew his job, and whose uniform was always sharp.

The next morning, I learned that even though I had been assigned a blue uniform, a white hat cover, white gloves, a Sam Brown pistol belt that I would be reporting for my first day of duty as an Air Policeman in fatigues a ridgeway cap, webbed pistol belt, and bloused boots. I reported to the flight line where the Air Policemen assigned to security duties at the base held their Guard mount, which amounted to an inspection, and passing along any information we needed to know about for duty during the upcoming shift. I was assigned to a flight with about fifty other Air Policemen. The assistant supervisor of the flight was Staff Sergeant Rapp, and I was assigned to ride with him and receive kind of an orientation. Staff Sergeant Rapp advised me that there were 300 Air Policemen in the 97th Combat Defense Squadron, which is what our Air Police Unit was called. He said out of those 300 Air Policemen, 25 were assigned duties as Sentry Dog Handlers. I knew almost immediately that was where my interests were.

Staff Sergeant Rapp filled me in on what Strategic Air Command was all about. The commanding general of the Air Force under President John F. Kennedy at this time was General Curtis LeMay. Staff Sergeant Rapp explained that SAC was the brainchild of General LeMay and was to be the United States Air Force solution to the Cold War and the Nuclear Threat which the United States faced. B52-Bombers would be on alert with Nuclear Weapons at Air Force Bases around the world 24/7. The Boeing build B-52 strato fortress is an American long range subsonic jet powered strategic bomber. It was introduced in February of 1955 and is still being used today. The B-52 is 159 feet long, has a wingspan of 185 feet, can travel at 650 miles per hour and has a range of 8,800 miles. It was built to carry nuclear weapons and can carry 70,000 pounds of armament. Two bombers at each SAC base would be in the air at all times. General LeMay was a seasoned Bomber Pilot from World War II and flew missions in Germany and Japan. He was the Air Force top no nonsense general. If you worked in SAC you had to deal with alerts and inspections on a regular basis. Later on I had seen a Time Magazine with General LeMay on the cover. He had kind of a stern look on his face and gripped a large cigar in his mouth. The caption on his photograph read, "The General the Russians Fear the Most." I learned from more experienced airmen that if you served in {SAC} you served with the elite part of the Air Force. SAC was always on alert and ensured the quality of their performance with regular surprise inspections. I was assured that the rest of the Air Force Commands were more relaxed, and laid back, and didn't go through all of these surprise inspections.

After a couple of hours, and during our shift, Sgt. Rapp drove me out to where the Sentry Dog Section was located. It was directly outside of a fenced area where all of the Nuclear Weapons were stored. The Sentry Dog Section had a fenced in area where there were dog houses sitting up off the ground about two feet on large steel posts. There was a steel ring attached to each post with a kennel chain that each dog was attached to. The dogs, attached to their chains, ran in a circle around their dog houses. The base had only been in operation for a couple of years, so the kennel facilities were temporary, until new facilities with individual kennel runs with concrete flooring would be built. As soon as we pulled up all the dogs began barking. Sgt. Rapp introduced me to T/Sgt. Rhodes who was the Kennel Master in charge of the dog section. He seemed like a big friendly guy, but I could tell he was highly squared away. His uniform was heavily starched and pressed to a crisp, and his boots were spit and polished. There was a building outside the kennel area which contained an office for T/Sgt. Rhodes, a kitchen area, a small meeting area with a table in the middle, and a bathroom. I mentioned to T/Sgt. Rhodes that I would sure be interested in becoming a dog handler one day. He took my name down and told me that I needed to be an Air Policeman for about six months, and he would get a hold of me when they had an opening.

All of the Air Force Sentry Dogs at Blytheville AFB were German Shepherds. I had done some research on the German shepherd dog and learned it was originally developed in 1889 by a German Army

Captain named Max Von Stephenitz. Captain Von Stephenitz was also a person who was in the sheep farming business and felt that a shepherd dog need not necessarily look beautiful, but instead needed to be intelligent, have the ability to work long hours and not get tired, and most importantly, needed to be protective toward his flock, and had to be courageous in order to fight off wolves. It was felt that because the Captain was also an army man that the appearance of the German shepherd was important primarily for the psychological impact the dog should have on criminal suspects or the enemy when used as a police or military dog. Over the years, the breeding both in Germany and America had caused slight changes in the appearance of the dog, but the natural protectiveness, courage, and intelligence remained. When World War II broke out, no one wanted anything to do with the word German, so the American German Shepherd Club changed the name of the breed and established the American Shepherd Club. In England, they changed the name of the German Shepherd to Alsatian. Several years after the war, the Americans changed the name back to the German shepherd, but it has only been recently that the English changed the name back.

I was enrolled in a couple of Air Police Correspondence Training Courses through what was called the U.S. Air Force-Air University. I received the rest of my training on the job. I was assigned to the Security Forces of the Air Police so I never really got to work in base law enforcement. Base law enforcement was the guys in the blue uniforms and white hats who worked the front gates, and were the uniformed police patrol on the base. The security forces protected the rest of the base, and primarily the alert aircraft, from sabotage. We wore army green fatigues, ridgeway caps, webbed pistol belts, and bloused spit shined boots. We were assigned duties as security sentries close to the aircraft, inside the fence. We carried 30 caliber Carbines from World War II. We walked around a B-52 Bomber on the alert pad for eight hours. As a SAC Base, seven 52 Bombers were parked on the end of the runway ready to take off on a moment's notice. That parking area was referred to as an alert pad. A supervisor, or Sergeant, would come around every couple of hours and bring coffee.

To my surprise, I had only worked as a Security Sentry for about two months when T/Sgt. Rhodes at the Sentry Dog Section asked me to come out for a meeting at the kennels because they had an opening.

I was definitely pleased to hear that my commander, Major William Haner had approved my transfer if I was interested. I was more than interested, and made it out to the Sentry Dog Kennels as soon as I got word. Sgt. Rhodes advised me that a Sentry Dog named "Chips" was becoming available to be re-trained with a new handler as his handler chose not to re-enlist and was being Honorably Discharged.

Chips was seven years old and had only worked with his former handler. I learned that he was named for a heroic and famous Army Sentry Dog from World War II who had captured a nest of enemy machine gunners, been wounded twice, and saved the lives of the men in his unit by detecting the enemy on several occasions. The World War II Chips was decorated for bravery by General Eisenhower himself, whom he almost bit during the ceremony. Later, the Army took back Chip's medals as they concluded that medals were not intended to be given to animals as in their view it cheapened the value and purpose of decorations. Fifty years later, in 2018, the World War II U.S. Army Sentry Dog Chips would be honored by the British with a medal created for heroic animals. Chip's original owner, was a young boy when Chips went off to World War II in 1942. Now, as a 76 year old man, Chip's owner and an American Military Working Dog accepted the medal posthumously.

Injured Gridder Bounces Back

1962

A Litchfield area youth, who just a year and one-half ago, lay near death from a serious football injury, has overcome the handicap of the injury, and now holds down a vital and interesting job with the United States Air Force.

A 3/c Andy Revering, son of Mrs. Eleanore Revering, Litchfield, enlisted in the U.S.Air Force in June, 1961, and now is a security sentry dog handler at the headquarters of the 97th Bombardment Wing at Blytheville AFB Arkansas.

In October, 1960, Revering, a lineman on the Litchfield high school team, suffered a ruptured large intestine while making a tackle in the Litchfield-Sauk Centre football game.

He was in critical condition for some time, and spent a long period of convalescence.

While in basic training, the injury bothered him considerably according to air force authorities, and he was offered a medical discharge, but turned it down, preferring to serve out his enlistment.

Revering was assigned to his duties as a security air policeman at Blytheville last August, and in May of this year took over the sentry dog "Chips."

These highly trained sentry dogs, which accompany the air

A3/C ANDREW REVERING AND "CHIPS"

policemen on their security rounds at the base, require careful and exact handling at all times, and Revering's task is regarded as one of the most demanding on the base.

My Chips was a pretty easy going and laid back Sentry Dog. He let me pet him almost immediately, with the offering of a little treat. Sgt. Rhodes advised me to just walk him around, talk to him, and pet him for the first week. He told me I should not give him any commands until into his second week. Working as a Sentry Dog Handler meant that you also had to put on the attack suit and perform as the aggressor in training the other dogs. I thought I had the best job in the world working with the greatest dog I ever had. I even enjoyed working as the aggressor in training the other dogs.

Into the second week Chips and I worked together like I was his original handler. I wasn't kidding myself. He had already been trained, and was really training me to work with him. He took all my commands to do obedience and agility work, and when we did attack work he came on really aggressive in protecting me. I couldn't have had a better dog. After three weeks of breaking in and training with Chips, Sgt. Rhodes said I was ready to be assigned to a shift and go on post. Security and Law Enforcement Air Policemen at the base worked three day shifts (7:00a.m.-3:00p.m.), three afternoon or swing shifts (3:00p.m.-11:00p.m.), and three night shifts (11:00p.m.-7:00a.m.), and three days off.

A/1C Andy Revering & Duke II guarding suspect

Air Force Sentry Dog Duke II apprehends suspect

Sentry Dog Handlers worked three swing shifts, three night shifts, and two days off. The dogs were considered to be of the most benefit during the hours of darkness. They could not be seen, but their special senses could detect any potential enemy or efforts to penetrate the base, or commit sabotage during the cover of darkness. Sentry Dog Handlers patrolled outside of the inner perimeter fence and in areas where they could not be seen by security lighting.

Airman Andy Revering puts Sentry dog Chips through training

On my first day of work with Chips, I reported for duty at the kennels at 3:00p.m, or 1500 hours military time. T/Sgt. Rhodes conducted a short inspection. While training with the dog section, I was made aware that dog handlers did not have to have spit-shined boots when reporting for inspection. That was required of the rest of the security and law enforcement forces, but they did all of their patrolling walking on concrete or in a vehicle. Dog handlers walked on patrol with their dogs in grassy field type areas. We still had to report in clean and pressed fatigues, but we could brush shine our boots. I liked that part, because I hated spit-shining my boots! We had six posts to man, so there were six dog handlers on a shift and one handler, who was at least an Airman First Class acting as the supervisor of shift. All of the posts surrounded the alert bomber area of the base except for one which was inside the fenced area of the Nuclear Weapons storage area. That area was right next to the kennels, so the handler who had that post on his shift simply walked over from the kennels to man it. To get to the rest of the posts, we muzzled our dogs and all climbed up onto a ¾ ton stake truck and were each dropped off at our post by the shift supervisor.

Circle Agitation and Gunfire Training

We didn't go on post until it got dark, so when we first came on duty we groomed our dogs and conducted some obedience, agility, and attack training. As soon as it got dark we were taken out to our posts and dropped off. Whatever area we were working we always zigzagged on foot patrol with our dogs walking into the wind. The dogs were trained to do open area scenting in order to detect anyone who may have penetrated our post. Every hour the shift supervisor would stop by with coffee, and we were allowed to sit in his truck for a few minutes to take a short break. It didn't matter how you preferred your coffee, it always contained cream and sugar. The supervisor would pick up a large thermos of coffee at the beginning of the shift at the Food Service Squadron, and apparently most guys preferred cream and sugar with their coffee, so that's the way you got it. I actually preferred my coffee black, but when I was on duty, I got used to coffee with cream and sugar To break up the monotony, and to insure the dogs were kept sharp in their duties, someone had to put on the entire attack suit and try to penetrate your post. We did this every two or three tour of duty, and everyone had to take their turn in the attack suit. I'll never forget the first time I did it.

U.S. Air Force Sentry Dog, Duke II

The whole attack suit is pretty heavy and you wear a cage over your head. When attempting to penetrate a handlers post you cannot see a thing as it is pitch dark. You just keep walking until you hear the handler challenge you. Soon a loud voice yells out, "Halt, who goes there?" You are not supposed to answer, but to just keep walking. After the third challenge, the handler sends his dog. The dog doesn't bark, and you don't see him, or even hear him, until he hits you. He bites whatever he comes to first, so he may get you in the leg, the arm, or the body of the suit. Some of the dogs hit you so hard that they knock you down! Soon after, the handler tells you not to move, and he has to run up and choke his dog off of you. Sentry dogs took a hard bite and didn't want to let go. To make sure that the dogs were not sleeve happy, or insure that the dogs would bite someone if they were not wearing and attack sleeve, we did muzzle training. We would put a leather muzzle on our dogs and another handler would have to run from the dog without an attack sleeve and the dog would attack him. If the dog was trying to bite the aggressor with the muzzle on, we were pretty sure he would bite without the attack sleeve. This was a bit of hazardous duty however, as sometimes the dog would bite through the muzzle. One time when I was performing duties as the aggressor, and taking hits from the dogs with muzzles on, I got bit through a muzzle. I was running away from one of the sentry dogs when he hit me right in the seat of my fatigue trousers, bit through the muzzle, and into my right buttock, and ripped my trousers right off, right down the seam lines. I had to take a short trip to the base hospital for some minor first aid, but we knew for sure, that sentry dog was definitely going to bite you if you weren't wearing an attack sleeve.

Dog handlers were not armed with 30 Caliber Carbines, but instead carried a handgun. Because the dog had to be physically controlled by the handler, it was felt that a handgun was the more practical weapon to be carried by K-9 handlers.

Firearms proficiency was part of our regular training as Air Policemen. The sidearm we were initially issued was the 45 Caliber Model 1911 Colt. It was a semiautomatic slide action handgun with a seven round clip. We were always required to carry it with an empty round in the chamber, which meant that if you were actually going to use it you had to pull the slide back with your weak hand and let it slam forward, which caused it to place a live round in the chamber and made it ready to fire. It was a very heavy sidearm and kicked like a mule when you fired it, which made it somewhat difficult to shoot accurately without a lot of practice. Virtually all of the armed forces carried this weapon.

In early 1962 all of our 45 Caliber Model 1911 Colt automatic handguns were replaced with the Smith & Wesson 38 Caliber Combat Masterpiece Revolver. I was never really given an explanation why the Air Force had chosen to replace the 45 Caliber Model 1911 Colt with the Smith & Wesson 38 Caliber Combat Masterpiece Revolver, but I learned later that General Curtis LeMay (Air Force Chief of Staff), was a competitive shooter, and determined that this was a more suitable weapon for the Air Police. Dog handlers in particular did not have to relinquish control of their dog while they engaged the use of their handgun. The revolver could be operated immediately with one hand, while still maintaining control of the dog with other hand. With the automatic you had to use your weak hand to pull the slide back, which caused the handler to temporarily lose control of his dog.

I personally liked the 38 Caliber Combat Masterpiece better than the automatic. It was lighter and did not kick as much when you fired it, requiring less practice to become accurate with it. I also appreciated the fact that I could immediately bring it into action with just one hand!

In June of 1962, I returned home to Litchfield on my first 30 day leave. When I returned from my leave I was advised by my supervisor, T/Sgt. Rhodes that Chips had passed away after having contracted heart-worms. At that time we had not yet found a cure for heart worms. Military veterinarians were using experimental drugs on our dogs, which we were told had some kind of poison in it, in an effort to kill the heart-worms. I always thought the medication was killing our dogs. Heartworms were carried by the mosquito, and Arkansas was full of them. Chips was already almost nine years old so I knew that he didn't have that much longer to work. The military did not have an adoption program for old or retired Sentry Dogs during this time, so if a dog simply could no longer perform their duties, they were put down.

T/Sgt. Rhodes advised me that he already had another dog for me to take over: a black and silver German shepherd named Duke I was available as his handler had gotten out of the Air Force while I was on leave. Duke was a pretty easy dog to take over. Duke was very intelligent, and his handler had been gone long enough, so that Duke was looking for someone to be friends with. He was so well trained that it was merely a matter of getting a couple of weeks of bonding together and we went right to work. Duke's former handler had also taught him several tricks, so he was most entertaining whenever we had to do a dog demonstration for high ranking personnel or other base community groups.

US Air Force Sentry Dog Duke I, my second dog

I was working an afternoon shift from 3:00p.m. to 11:00p.m on October 16, 1962, and had just reported for duty when we were advised that the base was going on full alert status, and the B-52 Bombers on the alert pad were getting ready to leave the base. We were further advised that this was not a drill nor a SAC Inspection, but an actual alert. We were told to load our dogs onto the ¾ ton truck as we were all heading out to our posts early. Normally we didn't go on post until it got dark. We were advised further that President Kennedy had placed all of the military on alert status because it had been discovered that Cuba was preparing nuclear warhead missiles for launch status, and that the missiles were provided by the Russians, who were refusing to remove them. All of the B-52 Bombers on the alert pad were armed with nuclear weapons, and all of these bombers had Russian targets.

We were dropped off at our various posts around the alert pad area of the base in broad daylight. As we were getting dropped off on our posts, the alert pad bombers began to leave, one after the other.

Shortly after the bombers left the base, all the KC-135 Tankers flew out also. The Boeing KC-135 stratotanker is a military Arial refueling aircraft. The KC 135 was the U.S. Air Force's first jet powered refueling tanker. The KC 135 first entered service with the Air Force in 1957. Now, we were walking around in these big open fields outside the fenced in area of the base, and there was nothing left for us to guard. All the planes had left. It was an eerie feeling to say the least, not knowing what may be coming next. Everyone was expecting this to end up being World War III or a Nuclear Annihilation. There wasn't much left to do, except to pray. We stayed in Defcon 2 status (Defense Readiness) for approximately 30 days. We worked the entire time for twelve hours on shift and twelve hours off. By the October 28, 1962, the Russians had agreed to pull their missiles out of Cuba, but we stayed on alert for another fifteen days. As a result of the Cuban Missile Crisis President Kennedy awarded the members of the 97the Bombardment Wing a Presidential Unit Citation with Oak Leave Cluster. A presidential unit citation had been awarded to the Air Force members of the 97th bombardment wings actions when it served in World War 11. The 97th bombardment wings in 1962 were all Air Force personnel serving at Blytheville Air Force base, when President Kennedy awarded the citation again with an oak leave cluster, which meant it was awarded for the second time.

The 97th Bombardment Wing had already been awarded this citation once before during World War II. The bombers and the tankers, that had left the base during the Cuban Missile Crisis, didn't return until we came off of alert status. It was a scary time!

I only handled Duke for about six months when he too became ill from heart- worm disease. Once again, I was convinced that the medication he was given was more deadly than the disease itself. Duke put up a heroic battle, but soon succumbed to his illness.

I was assigned maintenance duties around the kennels for a short period of time until another handler was honorably discharged after his four years of service. This time, a large reddish colored German Shepherd named Duke II, became available for me to take over.

ANDREW C. REVERING

Airman First Class Andy Revering and Air Force Sentry Dog Duke II

He was the most aggressive of all 25 dogs in our unit. To top it off, this dog seemed to have hated me the most. We had always been encouraged by our trainer, (when we walked through the kennel area to pick up after our own dogs) to agitate the other dogs to keep them aggressive. I use to poke at Duke I with a rake or shovel handle, get him to grab hold, and play tug of war with him. One time when he let go and I shoved it back at him I accidentally knock out two of his top front teeth. He never really forgave me for that, and literally hated my guts.

During the month I was trying to break in with him, I walked around with him, on the end of a snare (a rope loop on the end of a long pipe), with him trying to bite me regularly. Finally, T/Sgt. Rhodes, the NCOIC (Sergeant in charge of the K-9 Section), told me I'd better get a leash on that dog soon, or he would give him to someone who could. That was all it took! I wasn't going to give up Duke II, and T/Sgt. Rhodes threat to take him away and give him to someone else emboldened me to lose my fear of that big red dog. I snapped a leash on him shortly thereafter and we marched off like comrades in arms. Well, sort of. Sometimes, when we would be on post, and I'd tell Duke II to do something, he'd reach over and grab my closest hand to him and hold it tight enough in his mouth so that I couldn't get it out. He didn't break the skin, but he held on just tight enough so that I couldn't pull loose. At the same time, he would look up at me and growl. My solution to that little exercise was to carry a piece of rubber hose snapped to my pistol belt.

U.S. Air Force Sentry Dog, Duke II

Every time he pulled that stunt again, I'd smack him between the ears with the rubber hose, and he'd be good for a few days, but he never really stopped doing it the entire time I handled him. We had a relationship sort of built on mutual stubbornness with each other. Other than that little problem, he was a great sentry dog to work with. He was always top notch with his obedience and agility, and came on like a lion during the attack phase of his training. He never missed anyone trying to penetrate our post at night.

Airman First Class Andy Revering and Air Force Sentry dog Duke II.

On November 22, 1963 I was sleeping in my room in the barracks after working the 11:00p.m. to 7:00a.m. shift the night before. A staff sergeant from the orderly room came by in the early afternoon, knocked on the door, to wake me up and said that President Kennedy had been shot, and that we were to all immediately get into our duty uniform and report to Guard mount. At Guard mount, we were simply told that the president had been assassinated, and we were immediately taken out to the Sentry Dog Section. At the dog section, we were advised by the Sergeant in charge to leash and muzzle our dogs because we were being taken to a distant post to protect the base. Under normal circumstances, we didn't go on post until night had fallen and were assigned specific posts around and outside the bomber alert area. On this day we were not only assigned posts around the alert area but in and around the entire base. Once again, our assignments were highly unusual as we were on these posts in daylight and nighttime hours. In addition, before we had even gotten to our assigned posts, the alert bombers had departed the base. These bombers all had Russian targets, so early on it was rumored the assassination of the president had been some kind of Russian plot.

We stayed on alert status, working twelve hours on and twelve hours off for almost 30 days.

As it eventually became clear that the assassination of the president was not a Russian plot, we returned to our normal duties, regular shifts, and normal days off.

In the early part of 1964, the local police chief from the Blytheville City Police Department came to the Base Commander and inquired as to whether the Air Force Base would assist the police department in training a police dog. I was contacted by the Sentry Dog Section Sergeant Clinton Shepherd who inquired if I would be interested in taking this on. It just so happened that the local police officer selected to be the new police dog handler was a friend of mine, who used to work with me in the Sentry Dog Section. His name was Chuck Miller. He had married a local City of Blytheville young woman. He had been honorably discharged from the Air Force about a year earlier, got on the police department and decided to stay in Blytheville to raise his family.

I was aware of the misuse of police dogs in 1963, when police were dealing with black segregation demonstrations in Birmingham, Alabama, and Cambridge, Maryland. I was a little concerned that because of the persistence of segregation in Arkansas during this period that police in Blytheville may lean toward improper use of police dogs. However, when my friend, Chuck Miller was selected to be the handler, those concerns were alleviated. Chuck was from Ohio, and I worked alongside him for two years before he left the Air Force and got on the police department. He didn't have a racist bone in his body.

Officer Miller had obtained a beautiful black and tan large male German Shepherd named "Rebel". The dog was a year and a half old, so he was the right age for training. Sentry dogs were trained to be aggressive toward anyone except their handlers. Police dogs cannot be that way. They have to be able to work around other officers and civilians without being constantly aggressive toward them. After getting Rebel's basic obedience taken care of, we worked a lot on teaching the dog to be aggressive only on command or when his handler was threatened.

We did a lot of building searches and scent work. Teaching the dog to track human scent left at a crime scene until he eventually became very proficient at both. Officer Miller and I went to the city jail and asked prisoners who were serving as trustees if they wanted to volunteer to lay tracks for us. I wanted the dog to have a variety of scents to track instead of just mine. Several prisoners volunteered to help us in this training.

Some of the prisoners were Caucasian, some were Mexican American, and some were African American. I instructed all of these trustees to walk out for about a mile and climb a tree so that when the dog found them, he wouldn't bite them. The handler would have him on a thirty foot leash, but I didn't want any accidental bites. The training worked well and all the trustees seemed to enjoy getting out of jail for a short time to help us. Police departments in the area already had a few police dogs working. Most of those dogs were pretty aggressive. Memphis, Tennessee, which was 50 miles East of Blytheville, Arkansas, had six dogs at this time, and West Memphis, Arkansas, had two dogs.

CHASE—Rebel, Blytheville Police Department's German shepherd, races to the capture of a fleeing "burglar" in a demonstration of the use of dogs in police work. Charles (Chuck) Miller, Rebel's handler, holds him on a long leash as A1C Andy Reverend of Blytheville Air Force Base's sentry dog section, acts the part of a flushed burglar. The demonstration, given yesterday to members of the Arkansas Rehabilitation Service's Project Action group, included tracking, attack and mob control and basic training commands. (Courier News Photo)

Airman Andy Revering assists in training police dog for the Blytheville Police Department.

Officer Miller and Rebel made a great team, and together apprehended several criminal suspects and prevented injury to police officers on numerous occasions due to Rebels presence. I had never received any reports or heard of any improper use of Rebel as a police dog.

In June of 1964, I came home to Minnesota on 30 days leave. While home on leave, I helped my mother out by tending bar, and cleaning up her Tavern. On the second weekend that I was home three young women appeared at my mother's tavern early on Saturday evening. Two of the young women I recognized from high school, and knew them to be juniors when I was a senior. Since I wouldn't be turning age 21 myself until December of 1964, I knew these young women were younger than I and made sure they were not served any alcohol. The third young women with them I did not recognize. She was very beautiful and I felt an immediate attraction toward her. It turned out that she was also a junior at the same high school where I was a senior in 1961. I learned that her name was Bonnie Kuehl and that she was actually in a business class with me, but I simply didn't remember her. In high school I was going pretty steady with another young lady, and I guess I wasn't paying much attention. I really couldn't figure out how I missed her, because she was beautiful. We dated a couple of times while I was home on leave, and began to date her regularly when I finally got out of the Air Force.

In the early part of 1965 I was approached by a Sergeant from base personnel about whether or not I was interested in re-enlisting, because my four years of service was up in June of that year. I was already an Airman First Class (three stripes) and he told me if I would re-enlist, the Air Force would give me a $1000.00 bonus, another stripe (to Staff Sergeant), and send me and my dog to this exotic land. I told him I wasn't interested, that my time was up, and I wanted to go home and get into local law enforcement. I didn't realize at the time that he was talking about shipping me and my dog to Vietnam. We hadn't heard much about Vietnam. I had a roommate who went Temporary Duty to Vietnam for 90 days in 1964. When I asked him what the heck Vietnam was and what he did over there, he said there wasn't much happening there and he did the same thing over there that he was doing here which was guarding airplanes. I learned much later that in the late summer and the fall of 1965, the Air Force was sending Sentry Dogs and their handlers in large numbers to Vietnam. They were highly effective in preventing sabotage against the air bases by the Vietcong and were also used on patrols with the army.

On December 4, 1966, an Air Force Sentry Dog named Nemo and his handler Airman 2nd Class Bob Thorneburg, were patrolling a cemetery near their airbase in Vietnam. Suddenly, Viet Cong forces ambushed them, leaving Nemo with a bullet wound that entered through his eye and out his mouth. Thorneburg managed to kill two enemy soldiers before being shot in the shoulder. Despite his horrible wound, Nemo continued to attack Viet Cong forces, buying precious time for his handler to radio in for backup. After Thorneburg fell unconscious, Nemo laid on top of him to shield him from further harm.

When help finally arrived, it took several service members to remove Nemo from his master's injured body. Because of his bravery, Nemo saved his friend's life that day, truly earning him the name "man's best friend."

After Nemo's injuries were treated he was returned to the United States where he went on personal appearances and his story was told in order to recruit more dogs to be trained for war duties in Vietnam. Nemo was eventually retired to Lackland Air Force Base to live out the rest of his life as an honored war hero. Upon his death, his kennel was no longer occupied, and served as a monument to this great Air Force Sentry Dog.

CHAPTER 3

BECOMING A LOCAL POLICE OFFICER

On June 4, 1965, I was Honorably Discharged from the U.S. Air Force. I drove back to my hometown of Litchfield and decided to take a couple of weeks off before looking for a job in local law enforcement. After working with Sentry Dogs for the past four years and assisting a local police department in training their own police dog, I decided I wanted to work in a police department that had dogs. I thought that if anyone would have police dogs in Minnesota, it would have to be one of the two largest city police departments in Minnesota, which was either Minneapolis or St. Paul. After writing to Minneapolis and St. Paul, I received letters from both police chiefs stating that neither one of them had police dogs. I then took a map of the Minneapolis/St. Paul Metropolitan area and wrote to all 64 metropolitan area police departments. None of them had police dogs either. I did get a letter back from the police chief of Anoka, Minnesota, who said that they didn't have police dogs either, but that if I was interested, they were going to be testing for police officers in two weeks. I decided I probably should go out and find a police job first and then pursue my goal of becoming a dog handler. At this time in Minnesota, police officer recruits took a written exam, and if they passed that, they went on to meet a three member oral board. The oral board usually submitted the top three candidates to the police chief for selection. A candidate had to be at least age 21, have a high school diploma, and no criminal record, and if selected by the police chief, had to pass a doctors physical examination. I had all the basic qualifications. I had only just turned age 21 in December of 1964, but I was always told I looked older for my age.

I showed up for the written examination in the community room at the Anoka City Hall at the end of July of 1965. There were 25 young men present to take the test. We were advised before taking the test that if we passed, we would be notified in about a week to return for an oral board examination. The City of Anoka was a Northern suburb of Minneapolis. I didn't know anybody there and had never been there before. I received a notice one week later that I had passed the written exam, and I returned for the oral board the first part of August 1965. The three members of my oral board, whom I did not remember at the time, turned out to be the police chiefs of Cities of Coon Rapids, Fridley, and Columbia Heights, all of which are cities within Anoka County, Minnesota.

The police chief at this time in Anoka was a soft spoken gentleman named Dave Hoagland. Chief Hoagland stood over six feet tall, was in excellent physical condition, and had the grip of a lumberjack when he shook your hand. He selected me after the testing and oral board to be the only police officer they were going to hire. He said the City had never done this before, but that they were allowing him to hire a police officer three months early to replace a Sergeant who was retiring in December of 1965. The idea was to have a new police officer on board and trained so that no time was lost in replacing Sergeant George Karkhauff, when he retired. Chief Hoagland told me if I passed my physical exam, I would began my duties on September 1st, 1965. Chief Hoagland asked me if I had any questions of him. I asked him if there was anyone in this town that I was not supposed to arrest. I had grown up in a very small town where politics was sometimes suspected of being played, so I had concerns. Anoka was about three times larger than my home town. Chief Hoagland did not hesitate. He said, "Nope, you can arrest anyone you want to; as long as you have cause." I was impressed with him right off the bat. He was an honest police chief, who didn't play politics, and expected you to play by the rules. I passed my physical exam and began my duties on September 1st, 1965.

Andy Revering, City of Anoka, MN rookie police officer.

Chief Hoagland had advised me that we had to provide our own firearms, but that the city paid $50.00 towards uniforms. He took me to a place called Uniforms Unlimited in St. Paul where I purchased two uniform trousers, three shirts, a jacket, cap, gun belt and holster. The $50.00 covered about half, and the rest was paid by me. I borrowed a 38 Cal. Smith & Wesson from my younger brother, Mick, who had a large collection of guns, until I was able to order a new handgun for myself. I immediately ordered a brand new Colt Python 357 Magnum 4inch revolver. The price new at that time was $95.00. Today, that same handgun is valued at $3,000-4,000 dollars. Colt stopped making the Python in 1999. The company began reproducing the Colt Python in January of 2020. The price of the newly produced Python will be $1,499 dollars.

The City of Anoka consisted of seven square miles and had a population of 10,000 in 1965. The police department had a sworn officer strength of 15 fulltime officers, one female clerical staff, and a police voluntary reserve unit of seven officers. The department also consisted of two marked police cars, and two unmarked cars. Police Headquarters was attached to City Hall. The police building also contained its own city jail, and its own police radio system. We had two radios in our police cars. One was an Anoka County Sheriff's County wide radio, and one was the city police radio. In 1965, the City of Anoka had the largest city police department in Anoka County. The city also had its own municipal judge, whose chambers were on the second floor in City Hall, and whose courtroom doubled as a city council chambers.

When Chief Hoagland and I returned from St. Paul, he took me into the City Manager's office where I was introduced to City Manager Rudy Johnson. Mr. Johnson had been in his position for several years and he swore me in as a City of Anoka Police Officer.

Chief Hoagland then took me back to the police department where I was introduced and turned over to Captain John Hall. The police department consisted of a police chief, captain, three sergeants, one detective and nine patrol officers. A sergeant and three patrol officers were assigned to each shift. When I started, there were actually ten patrol officers as I was hired four months early to replace Sergeant George Karkhauff on the C-Shift (11:00p.m-7:00a.m.). Captain Hall advised me that I was being assigned to work Sergeant Karkhauff's shift along with Officers Art Erickson, Mike Auspos, and Frank Moinicken. I was assigned to ride along and receive on the job training from the officers on the C-Shift. During my first week on patrol on my own, I received a radio call at 12:35a.m. to check out a car that what was reported to have crashed into a telephone pole in front of the Clarke Service Station on West Main Street. Upon arrival I found a vehicle wrapped around the pole as reported. The engine was still running, steam was coming out from under the hood and the driver was still behind the wheel. I immediately went over to check on the driver for injuries and found him to be the only person in the vehicle. The driver appeared to be unconscious or sleeping as I approached him, but when I touched him on the shoulder, he woke up and looked at me with bloodshot sleepy eyes. I could detect a strong odor of alcohol about him and asked him if he was injured. He said he wasn't injured and I couldn't see any visible signs of any injury. I asked him if he would like to try and step out of the vehicle. I could see that he was very unstable on his feet, and appeared to be heavily intoxicated to the point where he would not be able to perform any field sobriety tests. I advised the gentleman that he was under arrest for driving while intoxicated, searched him and placed him the back seat of my squad car. When another squad car showed up take care of towing the vehicle in, I took the driver down to the police department and booked him into the city jail. I learned from another officer while booking him, that he happened to be the sports editor for the local newspaper and was a popular person in the city. He later plead not guilty to charges and went to court in front of the city municipal judge. While I was testifying against him on the witness stand, his attorney asked me, "What qualifies you to determine that this man was under the influence of alcohol? Have you even been to police rookie school yet?" I told the defense attorney that, "No I hadn't been to rookie school yet, but I grew up in a beer tavern." The defense attorney said, "No more questions your honor". The judge said, "I see why you don't have any more questions, and find the defendant guilty." On October 10, 1965, I began rookie school. Rookie school was four weeks long and was taught by the State of Minnesota, Bureau of Criminal Apprehension. Anoka Officer Rudy Betlach and I went to rookie school together. Officer Betlach had been hired two weeks before me. I would pick Rudy up at his house, or he would pick me up at my rental place, and we would travel to rookie school each day together. Rudy always reminded me that he had given up a pretty good paying job at Federal Cartridge Company in Anoka to take the job as a city police officer. Rudy had a large family, but his wife worked outside the home, and he always wanted to be a police officer. Rudy was a Navy veteran, grew up in Anoka, knew a lot of the local citizenry, and knew the city like the back of his hand. He had life skills, and had been in the police reserve unit, so I always knew he would really make a good police officer.

Almost immediately upon beginning my career with the Anoka Police Department, I continued to date Bonnie Kuehl. Bonnie was working as a secretary in a law office in Minneapolis at the time. It wasn't long after we began dating that we fell in love, became engaged and married on October 1st, 1966. Shortly after, Bonnie took a job as a secretary in a law office in Anoka. Initially, we lived in a rented basement of a small home in Anoka, owned by the widowed mother in law of an Anoka Police Sergeant.

I had only been working on the police department for less than two years when Captain John Hall approached me about becoming Anoka's first police dog handler. I had been lobbying Captain Hall about the value of police dogs for some time. Captain Hall was second in command at the police department. He told me he had received a flyer in the mail from something called the National Police Dog Academy in Moline, Kansas. He said further that this entity contended that they fully trained police dogs at their facility, and that handlers came down and spent two weeks breaking in with the dogs and would return to their agencies. The total cost to the agency for the dog and the training was $750.00. Captain Hall was proposing to raise the money for the new police dog by contacting a few of Anoka's community organizations. He eventually contacted the Anoka Jaycees, Anoka Lions Club, and the Anoka American Legion, who each agreed to contribute one third of the cost. I was later advised that Chief Hoagland had discussed this idea with neighboring City of Coon Rapids Police Chief Pat Nelson, who also wanted to send an officer to this training and to return with a trained police dog. Chief Nelson intended to come up with the cost of training out of his present department budget.

Within a couple of weeks, I was introduced to a Coon Rapids Police Officer named Leroy Anderson, who was to accompany me to the National Police Dog Academy in Moline, Kansas. I learned that Leroy was a U.S. Marine Corps veteran and had only been a police officer in Coon Rapids for less than a year. He was married and had five children, and never owned or had a dog in his life.

CHAPTER 4
A DOG NAMED DUKE

In the last two weeks of January 1967, Leroy Anderson and I left for Moline. We traveled down to Kansas in a newer model City of Coon Rapids Ford Station Wagon. Leroy drove the first few hundred miles and I drove second half of the trip. I remember driving across the plains of Kansas and took note of how flat the countryside was, and how you could see for miles. The speed limit was 65 MPH and I was driving about 70MPH. Far off to my right I noticed a small single engine airplane and commented to Leroy about the possibility of that being a State Trooper. His remark back to me was that we were the only vehicle on the roadway, so why would they be out here. A short time later, I noted a motor vehicle coming at a high rate of speed on a dirt side road and heading toward us. I said, "You don't suppose that is a State Trooper and that airplane was clocking us." A few seconds later, red lights began flashing on top of that vehicle. He was pulling us over. When the Trooper approached our vehicle he took note of our uniforms in the back seat and inquired if we were police officers. I told him we were police officers from Minnesota and looking for a town called Moline, Kansas where were to attend the National Police Dog Academy. He said he never heard of Moline, Kansas, but looked it up on his map and gave us detailed directions. He said he was just giving us a warning about the speeding, but to please slow down and have a safe trip. We were probably one hundred miles from Moline at that point, but the fact that the Trooper had never heard of this place caused us some concern. Now we weren't sure what we had gotten ourselves into. We arrived in Moline a couple hours later and quickly learned why even the State Trooper had not heard of this place. We discovered that the town consisted of a service station, general store, a church, and only a few houses. When we stopped at the service station and asked for directions to the National Police Dog Academy, the gentleman we spoke to said he had never heard of it. We then gave him the name of the person who was listed as the owner. The service station attendant advised us that he lived on a farm about a mile and one half outside of town and gave us directions. We drove on out to this farm and it did turn out to be the place we were looking for. The place appeared to be more of a small farm with a large two story house. I noticed about six dog kennels and what appeared to be a small obstacle course. The owner met us as we drove in and took us inside the house and showed us to our rooms. That evening, we had dinner served by the owner's wife, and he gave us a brief overview of the training we would be doing with our assigned dogs for the next two weeks.

On Monday morning, we were assigned our dogs. I was given a large, long haired, black and tan male German Shepherd named Duke, and Leroy was given a bit smaller male black and silver German Shepherd named Tag. Both dogs seemed very docile and easy to get along with. We took the first couple of hours to bond with them and let them get used to us. The trainer advised us that both dogs had already been trained in obedience, agility, and patrol dog work. Our role in the next two weeks was to continue bonding with the dogs and work them in what they had been trained to do. The trainer further advised us to give the dog's phony names as a precaution. He said that the way the dogs could not be called by strangers and would only respond to their handlers.

The two weeks went by pretty quickly and although I was concerned, I didn't say anything about the fact that we had done no gun work with the dogs and very little aggression training. Leroy, myself, and our dogs, Duke and Tag, graduated from the National Police Dog Academy on February 4th, 1967, and immediately began our trip back to Minnesota.

Coon Rapids Officer Leroy Anderson & Tag and
Anoka Officer Andy Revering & Duke

The woman who owned the home where Bonnie and I rented the basement apartment allowed me to build a kennel and dog house in the back yard, so I had adequate facilities to keep Duke.

The first week that we were back in Anoka, I advised Captain John Hall of what the trainer said about giving the dogs a phony name. Captain Hall was a fan of a 1950's television show called Sergeant Preston and Yukon King. It was the story of a Northwest Canadian Mounted Policeman and his Police Dog, King. He thought we should name our new police dog King. I agreed, as I too was a fan of the show. When Officer Anderson explained the phony name concern to his chief, he suggested to Anderson that they should name their dog Sarge. We learned in our own training that it didn't make any difference what the dog's name was. If they were trained properly in obedience, they wouldn't respond to anyone except their handlers anyway. It wasn't long after we had returned from police dog training when the Chief asked me to put on a presentation of the new police dog's performance and training for the Mayor, and the leaders of the various civic organizations who had funded the program. We journeyed out to the Anoka County Fair Grounds, which is on the North side of the city. It was still winter, so high snow banks were on each side of the roadway leading into the Fair Grounds. I gave a short verbal presentation about the use and value of police dogs and began to demonstrate the apprehension training the dog was taught. Leroy Anderson played the role of the bad guy, and took off running with the attack training sleeve on his arm. I immediately sent King in pursuit, but about halfway through the chase King veered off toward a snow bank, climbed half way up, lifted his leg, and urinated! Upon completion he took up the pursuit again and apprehended Leroy. The clear message I took home from that exercise was that you always remembered to empty your dog before performing any demonstration, so we taught our dogs to empty on command. Needless to say the police chief never let me forget about that event. He told that story on a regular basis!

Leroy and I began in-service training with our dogs almost immediately upon our return. We used the Anoka County Fairgrounds for our training area. The Fairgrounds were ideal as it was close, had several buildings on the property that we could use for building searches, and large open areas we could use for obedience, apprehension, and tracking training. One of the first things I wanted to check out in training was the dog's reaction to gunfire. We hadn't done any gun work in the training school and that worried me. Shockingly, we discovered when we began the gun training that both dogs were gun shy and Sarge wouldn't attack on the attack sleeve with any aggressiveness. Leroy had never handled a dog before in his life, and had not even had one as a pet growing up, so he was truly concerned. I advised him that we couldn't take the chance of telling the Chiefs about this problem, as they may well stop the K-9 program completely. I assured Leroy that I had experience in this area and that we would bring these dogs around. All of the dogs I had worked with in the Air Force were hard on the attack with gunfire and none of them were gun shy, so I actually had no experience at the time with gun shy dogs. I just had a strong feeling that if we started them out with really small caliber blank ammunition, such as a 22 Caliber fired at a distance, and then immediately distracted the dogs by agitating them with the attack sleeve, we could cure them of the gun shyness. We began by having a third person fire a 22 Caliber blank about 70 yards away, then immediately after the round went off, Leroy would agitate my dog with the attack sleeve and King would bite onto it. That seemed to work really well. When we tried the same thing with Leroy's dog Sarge with me as the aggressor; it did not go as well. Sarge was simply not aggressive and didn't want to bite the sleeve. It became clear quickly that Sarge was going to need a little more intensive agitation work to make him appropriately aggressive and wanting to bite on command. I had Leroy grab Sarge up close on his leather collar and told him to hang on tight. I grabbed Sarge by his tail and began pulling on the short hairs on the flanks of his back legs. He came unglued very suddenly, wanted to bite me, and showed the kind of aggression I was looking for. We tried the gunfire with him again, the same way we did with King and this time he did just fine. Within a week, we changed from 22 Caliber blanks to 38 Caliber blanks, and later to 45 Caliber blanks, and eventually the shotgun. Gradually, we moved closer to the dogs as the guns were fired and soon were able to fire off a weapon in one hand while holding the attack sleeve and taking the bite from the dog in the other. Both dogs now knew that when a gun went off, there was nothing to fear and they became aggressive. Later the dogs were trained to ignore the gunfire when the gun was being fired by their handlers.

CHAPTER 5
A DOG NAMED KING

In March of 1967, King and I were working the dog watch shift which was 11:00p.m. to 7:00a.m. We were on patrol doing security checks of various businesses on the East side of the city when we discovered a broken window on the back overhead garage door of a local gas station. There was only one patrol vehicle available to assist us, and that was being used by my supervisor, Sergeant Art Erickson. While the Sergeant covered the front of the building, I yelled in a warning through the broken window: If there is anyone inside come out! I have a police dog and will send him inside in two minutes! When there was no response, I broke the rest of the glass out of the window so that King would not get injured when he entered, and sent him in. He stiffened and began to growl when he entered the building, so I knew immediately that there was someone inside. I followed King through the window and he went immediately to the office area of the service station, leaped behind the counter and grabbed onto a hidden suspect. I called out to the suspect, as King had hold of him by the leg and was dragging him back toward me, and told him if he had any weapons that he should drop them. He cried out that he did not have any weapons and to please call off my dog. I then had the suspect lean against the wall and spread his feet to be searched. I advised him that my dog would be watching him while I searched him and if he tried to escape or to attack me that the dog would bite him again. He stood quietly against the wall while King watched him and I searched him. We then escorted him out the front door, which I was able to unlock from the inside, and placed him with handcuffs behind his back in the front seat of my squad car. I put King in behind him in the back seat, and told him if he tried to escape or assault me, the dog would attack him. There was no screen between the front and back seat, so King would put his nose in the back of the suspect's neck and growled at him all the way to the City Jail.

Anoka Police dog King and Officer Andy Revering, 1967.

In the first few months that King and I worked together we did not have a specific squad car assigned to us. When we came on duty we would take one of the marked cars that an officer had used from a previous shift, take the lower part of the back seat out, and put in a three quarter inch plywood platform with some rubber padding. In the early 1960's, we had no screens between the front and back seat to keep prisoners from assaulting officers, and therefore no screen that separated the police dog in the backseat from jumping into the front seat. With the police dog, that was also important for traffic stops. Whenever a vehicle was pulled over, the front driver's window was always left down, the dog would jump into the front seat and lean out the window where he could watch while the officer dealt with the offender. If the offender became assaultive or tried to run away, the dog would jump out of the window and come to the aid of the officer. We trained the dogs regularly in prisoner transportation and to come without being commanded if the officer was in trouble.

One morning not long after King and I had started working together, the chief's unmarked car was in the shop, and a swing shift officer was giving the chief a ride home. The chief happened to be riding in the squad car normally used by the police dog handler when he was on duty. The officer giving the chief a ride home wanted him to have an understanding of what happens to a car used regularly with a police dog in it. The officer escorting the chief pulled the air vents open as he drove the chief home and a dog hair dust storm blew from under the seats and all over the chief's handsome new suit. The next day, the chief assigned his unmarked police car permanently to the police dog handler, and made arrangements with the city manager to be paid a monthly stipend for him to use his privately owned vehicle for work.

In early March 1967, King and I were working the dog watch. I pulled into Ember's Restaurant on South Ferry Street at 3:00a.m. for a lunch break. In the parking lot right next to my vehicle was an older model beat up car that I recognized as belonging to an elderly woman whom I recognized as Henrietta O'Malley. Henrietta had a large older Victorian home on South Ferry Street about two blocks from Ember's Restaurant. Henrietta could best be described as kind of a harmless night person. As I started to get out of my vehicle I saw Henrietta get out of her vehicle at the same time and approach me. The window on my vehicle was rolled halfway down and King had his head out and was barking and growling at her as she approached me. Henrietta said to me, "Andy, I very much like your dog and am going to pet him." Before I could say anything back to her, she walked right over to King and patted him on his head. He immediately stopped barking and growling and let her continue to pet him. Henrietta was not the most put together person. She had stringy unkempt red hair, and baggy clothing which didn't always look that clean, and at times she had a kind of distasteful odor about her. King didn't care! He liked her, and she was the only person he ever allowed to pet him in this manner. We would routinely run into Henrietta in the middle of the night over the years and she would always walk up and pet King and talk to him.

Many years later, in about 1997, long after Henrietta had passed away, when I had been promoted to police chief, a young woman came to visit me in my office. She was a doctor from California and was Henrietta's daughter. She wanted to know if I was the same Andy Revering who handled a police dog named King back in the 1960's, who let her mother pet him. She wanted me to know that her mother always spoke very highly of the young police officer and his dog from Anoka who always treated her kindly. I told her that yes I was that officer and was proud to have known her mother all those years. I never knew Henrietta O'Malley had a daughter and this meeting was very special to me. It brought back a lot of very fond memories of an old, lonely, night woman who was comforted by a big friendly police dog.

In the latter part of March 1967, King and I were working the dog watch, when we received a radio call at 2:00 a.m. to proceed to the Anoka State Hospital. There was someone on top of a water tower at that location with a rifle, and he stated that he wanted to shoot a police officer. Officer Mike Auspos, who was the senior officer on duty, was in another squad car and he too was responding to the call as well. Mike was a former U.S. Marine and an experienced police officer. His dad, Mike Auspos Senior, was the former Anoka County Sheriff, so Mike Jr. had been around law enforcement all of his life. Mike advised me to respond to the location with no headlights so that the rifleman would have less chance of seeing us. We had kill switches in our vehicles for the tail lights, brake lights, and head lights, so that we could make an approach at night without being seen beforehand. Unfortunately, there were street lights all the way around the circular drive at the Hospital, so immediately upon exiting our vehicles, shots rang out and bullets were hitting the ground next to where we stood. I grabbed King's leash and we headed for cover behind a large oak tree. Mike also sought cover. A couple more shots rang out as we sought cover, and I heard the bullets hitting the ground around us. We could not see anything at the top of the water tower because it was pitch dark. We also didn't want to fire blindly at a shooter we couldn't see, as we were afraid of shooting holes in the water tower. Mike yelled up at the shooter that we were the police and that he should throw the gun down and surrender. That was met with a couple more shots toward us. About twenty minutes later, a psychiatrist who worked at the State Hospital arrived on the scene. He said that he knew who the youth was on top of the water tower and that he was going to go up and bring him down. Mike told him to go ahead. Not long after the psychiatrist climbed up the water tower, we heard him yell that he had the youth's rifle and was going to toss it to the ground. We heard the thud as the rifle hit the ground and shone our flashlights on it, just to be sure. Shortly thereafter the psychiatrist came down with the youth in tow, whom he said was one of his patients from the Youth Center at the State Hospital. He said he would be taking the youth back to the State Hospital. Mike Auspos advised the psychiatrist that the youth would be going with us to jail, and that he was under arrest for aggravated assault. This was my first experience with being shot at on the job. I was most impressed with the way King reacted. He was definitely not gun shy, and each time the youth shot at us he growled and became aggressive, pulling on his leash and wanting to go after him. King did well under fire! A couple days later, I was on my days off and when I went out to feed King in the morning he was gone from his kennel. I kept a padlock on the kennel which was still locked, and the surrounding fence was six feet high, but it had no fence on top. My heart about stopped when I found him gone from his kennel. I really believed that King could not climb out of that kennel, but it was becoming quickly clear to me that is what he did. I began looking around the neighborhood and calling his name with no response. On the North side of the street that we lived on was a manufacturing company called Cornelious Thermo Serve. They manufactured insulated coffee jugs, cups, and mugs to keep liquids warm. A large parking lot was next to the entrance to their building right across the street from where we lived. When I looked in that direction, I could see that people were beginning to enter the building for the work day. I also took note that before each person entered the building they bent down and patted a big black looking dog who was sitting by the front door. The front door to the Cornelious Building was about 100 yards from where I was standing in my yard. I strained to look closer when it hit me that the dog greeting everyone at the entrance door was King. I walked slowly toward the building, and as

I got within 20 feet of the door, King noticed me and began wagging his tail and ran up to greet me. I chose to not discipline him at all as I was grateful that he hadn't bitten anyone, and I simply walked him back home. The message came home clearly to me that this dog knew the difference between good guys and bad guys, and if that if I didn't command him to apprehend someone or no one was threatening me he would not bite them. I did begin immediately to put a top on his kennel so that he couldn't climb out again.

Andy & Bonnie Revering and King

In early April of 1967, King and I were on patrol and doing our security rounds in the city. At 2:30a.m., we drove through the Main Motors Chevrolet/Cadillac Dealership and observed someone running from the back of the body shop area. I slammed my patrol vehicle to a stop, got out and yelled for this individual to halt and that I was a police officer. When he kept running, King was sent to apprehend him. I took off on foot behind King, and could see the shadow of his figure leaping over various articles while he was in pursuit. I didn't realize until a short time later that these articles were various discarded auto parts from the body shop. Moments later I heard King give out a yelp, and saw him coming back toward me walking slowly on three legs with his right front paw held up. As he got closer to me I could see that he was bleeding heavily from a two inch gash between the knuckle and elbow of the paw he was holding up. I could see that he was hurt badly. I was scared! I picked him up immediately and ran back to my patrol car and radioed the dispatcher to call Dr. Norm Epping at the Coon Rapids Pet Hospital, and to advise him that I was on the way with an injured police dog. I knew that Dr. Epping lived right next to the Pet Hospital and he would be quick to respond. I then got out my first aid kit and wrapped bandage gauze around King's leg tightly in the form of a tourniquet to stop the bleeding, before heading off to the Pet Hospital. I placed King in the front seat next to me, so that I could keep my right hand around the bandaging and further prevent the bleeding. I talked to him softly, and told him everything was going to be ok. He looked up at me with those soulful eyes and appeared comforted as we sped to the Pet Hospital. Dr. Epping met me at the door of the Pet Hospital when we arrived, and I carried King inside and lay him down on the exam table. I explained to Dr. Epping what had happened and he gave King an injection and then immediately got to work stitching up his wound. The doctor then bandaged the wound and advised me to bring King back in two days so that he could check for any infection. He said the dog should not return to work for at least three weeks. King made a full recovery in three weeks and although the leg was still a little tender, he no longer limped on it, and he returned to work.

My wife Bonnie and I had been busy trying to have a child for the past couple of years. We had become somewhat concerned that it was not going to happen, when in May of 1967, she announced to me that she had seen Dr. Matt Yelle, our family physician, and was advised that she was pregnant. We were both very happy! The little basement apartment we were living in only had one bedroom so we began looking for a home for us to buy.

CHAPTER 6
KILLED IN THE LINE OF DUTY

King and I were again working the dog watch on June 10, 1967, when at about 2:00a.m. we received a radio call from Sergeant Jim Sampson of the Anoka County Sheriff's Department. He asked me if I could respond to a request for assistance from the St. Francis Police Department, who were in a field in their city and involved in a shooting. Sgt. Sampson said both he and the only other Anoka County Sheriff's Patrol Vehicle on duty were on the opposite end of the County and out of position to respond quickly, but were on the way. I advised Sergeant Sampson that I could respond immediately. The City of St. Francis was located ten miles, north of the City of Anoka on Hwy 47. St. Francis was patrolled by a part time police chief named Gerald Boos, whom I knew personally, and reserve police officers. Gerald Boos was a good friend of Anoka Police Officer Rudy Betlach. They had both went to Anoka High School, and were in the same graduating class. Gerald Boos was 29 years old. While en-route to the scene I was in radio communications with the St. Francis Police Reserve Officer who was working that evening with Chief Boos. He advised me of his exact location which was in a field just off of Hwy 47, about a mile from there central city area. I arrived within ten minutes, as I was proceeding with red lights and siren. When I pulled into the field behind the St. Francis Patrol vehicle, I noted the police reserve officer was standing behind the open driver's door, and that he was holding a shotgun. About twenty feet in front of him were about fifteen teenage young men and women who were standing outside of three or four vehicles. The reserve officer had his headlights and spotlight shining on these youth, who were showing signs of being under the influence. I approached the reserve officer and asked him where Jerry was and what had happened. He said he was not sure where Jerry was right now. He said when they pulled into the field they heard what sounded like firecrackers going off, or gunshots. He said Jerry got out of their patrol vehicle when they arrived and told all of the youth to get back into their vehicles. He said at that point, two of the youths began to run away and Jerry went after them. He said he heard shooting, and had not heard anything from Jerry since. I told him I would take King and see if we could locate him. I hooked up King to his 30 foot tracking leash, and had him try to get a scent from around the St. Francis Patrol vehicle where Jerry was seated. King took off in a straight line north of the vehicle. As he jumped over a downed tree, he apparently banged the wound on his right front leg, and let out a yelp, before proceeding. About twenty feet from the St. Francis patrol vehicle, Chief Boos was located face down in some weeds. I checked him for a pulse and he had none. He appeared to have been shot twice, from the wounds I observed. I felt a sense of fear, and anger at the same time! My immediate reaction was to begin searching for the shooters. I knew I could not leave the scene as only a reserve officer was present, and we didn't know the involvement of the teenage youth still present, or if the shooters weren't among them. Shortly thereafter Anoka County Sheriff's Patrol Sergeant Jim Sampson arrived and took charge of the scene.

The reserve officer advised Sergeant Sampson what he had observed, and I advised him about the location of Chief Boos body. Sergeant Sampson advised me that he had ordered a bus be sent to this location, and asked me if I and my dog would get on the bus and escort the teenagers who were on the scene to the Anoka County Jail. Investigators needed to sort this all out. Sergeant Sampson advised me further that he would have another deputy drive my vehicle back to the County Jail. I told Sergeant Sampson, no problem, King and I would take those kids to jail. All of the teenagers at the scene were searched by deputies and herded onto the bus. They were loud and obnoxious until King got on the bus with me, and growled at them a couple of times. After that, none of them created any problem on the way to the County Jail. I learned later that two teenage brothers began shooting at Chief Boos when he advised all of them to return to their vehicles. He returned fire from his service revolver. In the exchange of gunfire both youths were wounded, but Chief Boos was killed. Chief Boos was survived by a wife, a son age four and a daughter age 3. As a footnote to this incident: Many years later when I became the Police Chief in the City of Anoka, I hired Chief Boos's then adult daughter as one of our first female police officers. She later went on to become a detective with the Anoka County Sheriff's Department Major Crime Unit.

On June 15, 1967, King and I were called to the Anoka State Hospital on a report of a patient in the Youth Center alleged to have assaulted a hospital staff person. We arrived at the State Hospital at the same time as an ambulance which had been dispatched to take care of the victim. Staff advised me that a patient in the youth center had broken a metal leg off of a table and used it to seriously assault a male member of the staff. The patient had barricaded himself in a room, refused to surrender his weapon, and would not come out. I was led down a hall with King to the room where the patient was barricaded. I spoke loudly to the patient inside the room. "I'm a police officer I have a police dog, and if you don't surrender your weapon and come out I will send the dog in." When I received no response I repeated my warning a second time. After receiving no response to the second warning, another officer helped me push the door in, and I released King inside the darkened room. I heard some growling, some thrashing and banging around, shortly I heard, "Ouch, Ouch, Get him off me, get him off me." I turned my flashlight on an observed that King had the youth by the arm, down on the floor. I immediately called him off and King stood guard on the youth while I searched him for any other weapons. He was then handcuffed and taken into custody. The next day I was advised by Captain John Hall that a State Hospital Psychiatrist complained to him about the police department putting dogs on youthful hospital patients. Captain Hall told me further that he advised this person that if the hospital did not like the way the police department handled patients who behaved criminally, they should not call us and deal with those situations themselves. Needless to say they didn't stop calling us on a pretty regular basis when they needed help. And those calls were pretty regular, as there was no security force at the State Hospital at the time.

On June 18, 1967, at 2:15a.m. King and I were on patrol and making our security rounds checking business for possible burglaries.

As we came around the back of a local service station we observed someone began to run from the back of a tire storage area. I yelled to the person to stop or I would send a police dog and the suspect immediately surrendered. I searched the suspect for weapons, handcuffed him and placed him in the front seat of my squad car under arrest for attempted burglary. There was no screen between the front and back seat and King would put his nose in the back of the suspect's neck and growl at him. I told the suspect if he tried to escape or attack me that the dog would bite him. He said he understood. I got King out of the car first when we got to the county jail and escorted the suspect inside. I stood by with King as the deputy in the jail strip search the suspect. To my complete surprise and shock, as the deputy pulled the man's jockey shorts down, a small fully loaded 22 caliber handgun fell to the floor. I had to have been standing there with my mouth wide open as the deputy picked the weapon up, handed it to me, and said, "I think you might have missed something." It was a lesson well learned. I always made sure I made a complete body search after that whenever I placed someone under arrest. I will never forget, a few years later when a police officer from the Columbia Heights Police Department when bringing a youthful prisoner up to the backdoor of the County Jail. The youth was handcuffed in the backseat of the officer's car, and there was a screen between the front and back seat. The youth had managed to get hold of a handgun which he had hidden in the back of his trousers, shot and killed the officer, and shot and wounded a deputy who came to the officers aid, before the youth was restrained. I am confident that the only difference in these two situations is the fact that I had a trained police dog with me watching the offender I was bringing in the whole time, and he was simply very afraid of the dog and didn't try to reach for the hidden gun.

On July 2nd, 1967, my supervisor, Sgt. Art Erickson advised me that there was a house for sale on Park Street just down the block from him. He said he felt sure it may be in our price range. A police officer's salary was only $450.00 a month at this time, but Bonnie worked full time, and I worked overtime whenever I could, so we thought we could handle purchasing our first home. We checked out the house. It was a two bedroom home with one bath, a full unfinished basement and no garage. The price was $13,900.00. Our monthly payment was $78.00 a month. I was a veteran so we would be able to obtain a VA Loan, which meant no huge down payment. We both liked the house, so we bought it. Shortly after we moved in, the city built a 10ft. by 12ft. cement dog kennel with chain link fence, and a beautiful dog house for King in my back yard.

On July 6th, 1967, at 1:30a.m. we received a call from the Minneapolis Police Department for assistance. One of their patrol cars had gotten into a chase with a stolen vehicle which crashed into another vehicle at Hennepin Ave. and 5th St. where the driver had fled on foot. I received permission from my supervisor to head down there and see if we could track the suspect. I advised Minneapolis Police while I was proceeding to their location, that it would take me about twenty minutes to get there, and to make sure no one got into or around the stolen vehicle as it may disturb the scent. Upon arrival I immediately hooked King up to his thirty foot leash and let him sniff inside the crashed stolen vehicle. He took off down the sidewalk on Hennepin Ave. pulling very hard on his leash. I kept telling him, "Find him boy, find him." Following behind us on foot were a Minneapolis Police Sergeant and five patrol officers. King went for two blocks down Hennepin Ave. took a right turn on a side street for another two blocks where he made a left turn down another street. He went for another block and turned and went up the front steps to an apartment building. I asked King, "Is that where he is boy, is he in there". He growled and scratched at the front door. The front door was unlocked when I pulled on it. We entered the lobby, and King pulled on his leash down a long hallway and stopped at a door near the end of the building. Again, I asked him. "Is he in there boy, is he in there." He looked up at me, looked back at the door and growled. The Minneapolis Police Sergeant asked me if the guy was in there. I told him, "Well, that's what my dog says." He immediately kicked the door in and he and the other five officers charged inside. They pounced on a black male sitting in a large chair in the front room. This gentleman had cuts and bruises about his head and hands. Injuries he could have sustained in a car accident. He did not resist the police officers and was taken into custody without incident. He was charged with auto theft and did have a criminal record. He later plead not guilty to the charges and I ended up having to testify at his trial as an expert witness as to the tracking effectiveness of my dog. Before the trial was completed he agreed to a plea.

On July 15, 1967, King and I had been working the Dog Watch when we received a call to report to the office and see the Sergeant. Upon arrival Sergeant Erickson advised me that he had received a phone call from the Wilmar, Minnesota Police Department. He said they had an armed robbery of a gas station about a half hour ago and police chased the suspect vehicle until it went into a ditch and the occupants fled into a corn field about a mile outside of their city. Wilmar was about 125 miles West of Anoka, and the Sheriff's Office out there was sending a light airplane to pick up King and me at the Anoka County Airport. He said they would be there within the hour. The sergeant said he had approved King and me going to assist them in their search, so I immediately left for the airport. I had never been on a light plane and I was sure King hadn't either. I was more concerned how he would react to it than how I felt about it. We no sooner got to the airport and the plane landed. The plane was even smaller than I had anticipated. It had two seats in front and a very small back seat. I lifted King up into the back seat. He immediately lied down and went to sleep. We had just worked the night before, so I guess I shouldn't have been surprised. The pilot of the plane was a volunteer member of the Kandiyohi County Sheriff's Department in Wilmar. I learned he was a farmer by trade, and that the plane belonged to him, and he didn't know much about the case, except that they called him to come and pick me up. We landed at the Wilmar Municipal Airport within the hour, and were picked up by a Sheriff's vehicle and transported to the corn field where the suspect vehicle was located. It was almost noon by the time King and I got on the scene. Deputies told me that they pretty much had the corn field surrounded by other deputies, reserves, and other volunteers. I snapped on King's thirty foot leash and allowed him to jump inside the suspect vehicle and sniff around for a scent. He came charging back out of the vehicle and headed straight into the corn field and appeared to be on the trail of the suspects. As we got further into the field it became obvious that he was on the trail, as I could see clearly two sets of footprints in the black soil surrounding the corn stalks as he proceeded at a steady pace, pulling hard on his tracking leash. We must have traveled about a mile and a half when we came out on the other side of the corn field. The two sets of tracks King appeared to be clearly following, appeared to end at a blacktop county road. We tried to pick up a trail both East and West on that road, but to no avail. All indications were that the suspects had to have gotten into another vehicle and fled the scene before the Sheriff's Department could get enough people in place to seal off the field. A Sheriff's vehicle picked us up on the other side of the field and transported us back to the airport. The pilot who flew us up to Wilmar was at the airport waiting to take us back to Anoka. I learned a few days later that Minnesota State Patrol Troopers had spotted a suspicious vehicle a few hours later, stopped it, detained the suspects, and learned they had captured the robbery suspects.

On September 12th, 1967, King and I received a call to report to the Anoka County Jail to assist deputies with an unruly prisoner. This was not an unusual request, as we had routinely assisted deputies at the jail in dealing with prisoners who were threatening to cause a problem. Normally we would show up, a deputy would open up the holding cell door, I would caution the prisoner to just do what the deputies wanted them to do. King would be at my side, and would growl at them, and they would comply. This time was different. I was advised that the prisoner in the tank was at a bar in the City of Columbia Heights, a community in Southern Anoka County, got into a fight with several patrons, and it took five officers to take him into custody, and bring him to jail. When the deputy opened up the holding cell door I could see that the prisoner had a very muscular build, and he was sitting on a bench in the tank. While King was sitting at my left side on a short leash, I advised the prisoner to just do what the deputies wanted him to do, and we wouldn't have any further problem. He immediately stood up, unbuckled and pulled a wide belt with western buckle off of his trousers, wrapped the belt around his right hand and said, "You go ahead and send that son of a bitch, I'll get one of you before he gets me." King began to growl and lunge at the man, but I could see that the prisoner was not afraid and didn't intend to do what I asked. Not wanting to see him get hurt, I took my small tear gas canister from my pistol belt, and while holding King tight on a short leash with my left hand, I began spraying the man with tear gas. I sprayed him directly in the face and chest area and he did not appear to be suffering any effects from the mace. He looked directly at me and said, "In case you haven't figured it out yet officer that stuff doesn't work on me." My first reaction to myself was, "what are we going to now, I really don't want to hurt this guy, and the tear gas isn't working", but in the next moment he sat down on the bench, reached up to rub his eyes, and the belt loosened up on his hand. It appeared to me he was in fact having a re-action to the effects of the mace, and was willing to surrender. I kept King on a short leash with my left hand and reached in with my right hand to take the belt from his hand. He quickly stood up and hit me across the face with the belt buckle. Temporarily stunned, I dropped the leash, and stepped back to cover my face from being struck again. King immediately jumped in and grabbed the prisoner in the area of his groin and took him down on the floor, pulling on the front of his trousers. I heard the man screaming, "Ouch, Ouch, Get him off me, get him off me," as King growled and tugged firmly on the bite hold he had. When I uncovered my face, and saw what was happening, I grabbed King's leash and called him off of the bite. As King released his bite hold, the prisoner immediately grabbed the dog by his upper lip with his right hand. He had the dog in such a tight grip that King was unable to get loose and bite him again. King was now screaming in pain from the grip this man had on him. The deputy who had opened the tank door began striking the prisoner in an effort to get him to release his hold on King. When he finally let go of King, the dog was angry and agitated, and jumped back in and grabbed him by the inside of his right leg and held him on the floor. Once again the man was screaming, "Get him off me, Get him off me." I called King off the bite and the deputy, King and I backed out of the holding cell and locked the door. When I looked back in the cell through the small window in the door, that prisoner looked up at me and said, "Are you guys ready to go another round?" He was pretty much the toughest guy I ran into on the job. We charged him with assault, and disorderly conduct. When this gentleman came before an older Anoka County Judge the following day he was sober and humble. The judge fined him, lectured him and threatened to lock him up and throw away the key if he saw him again.

On October 12, 1967, I received a call at home from Coon Rapids Police Sergeant Dick Super. Coon Rapids was a neighboring community on our Eastern border. He said they had not been unable to get hold of their K-9 officer Leroy Anderson and needed King and I to assist them with a building search at Shoppers City. Shopper's City was a large shopping center similar to Target or Walmart stores. I had been aware that a Coon Rapids undercover officer by the name of Buck Shepherd, had information through an informant, that two parolees from Stillwater State Prison planned on hiding inside Shoppers City, and when they closed at 6:00p.m., they intended to burglarize it. I knew Buck Shepherd personally, as he worked the dog watch the same time I did, and we sometimes worked cases together that crossed city boundaries. I considered him to be an experienced and competent police officer. Buck had given the information he had received about the intentions of the two parolees to the Coon Rapids Police Chief. He further advised the chief that his informant made it pretty clear that these two guys would be armed and did not intend to be taken alive. The Chief authorized overtime for Buck, two other detectives, and K-9 officer Anderson to stakeout the Shopper's City for two weeks. When the burglars didn't show up he discontinued the overtime. Buck continued to stakeout Shopper's City on his own time and observed the two parolees enter the building. He did not see them leave. Buck advised the on duty Sergeant Dick Super, who called in other officers and tried to get hold of their K-9 Officer. That's when I was called. Upon arrival at the Shopper's City I was met by Sergeant Super, and Officers Dale Yonker, and Don Sergeant. I knew all of these officers personally as they all worked the Dog Watch in Coon Rapids and I would see them regularly in the course of our duties. Sergeant Super advised me that my dog King and I would go in to search the building, and that Officers Dale Yonker and Don Sergeant would come in behind me as back-up. Both Officers Yonker and Sergeant were armed with shot guns. We entered the building through the front doors. All the lights were still on inside the building, but we were advised that all employees and customers were no longer inside. As we entered the front doors there was a stairway immediately to the right which went up to a balcony area that surrounded the main area of the store. It was a furniture department. King started up the stairs right after we entered the building. I stopped him and unsnapped his leash so that he could search without being held back. He went into the second bay area which contained a couch, coffee tables, and wall cabinets.

King captures prison parolees inside Shopper's City
Complex, who said they wouldn't be taken alive.

He went immediately behind the couch and grabbed hold of the
first suspect by his jacket and dragged him out to where we were cov-
ering him. Officers Yonker and Sergeant placed him in handcuffs and
Yonker took him back outside to waiting officers. I sent King back
in to search further and he went over to a large dining room cabinet
in a corner of the room, jumped up on it and began barking. I called
him back and snapped his leash back on, and from cover yelled into
the room, "this is the police, come out of there with your hands in
the air, or we blow that cabinet to pieces!" This suspect yelled back,
"I've got a gun." I yelled back to him, "throw the gun out, push that
cabinet over, and come on out keeping your hands where we can see
them." In the next second a handgun, revolver type, came flying out
over the top of the cabinet. Shortly thereafter the suspect pushed the
cabinet over and crawled out. Officer Sergeant took him into custody. As Officer Sergeant walked out the front door with the second
suspect in handcuffs, King and I were right behind him. I noticed
the Coon Rapids K-9 Officer driving through the parking lot in his
private vehicle with his whole family in the car. He never forgave me
for stealing these two felony suspects away from him. I advised him
that he had to make sure his agency was more aware of where he
was when he wasn't on duty. This was long before such things as cell

phones, so it was not as easy to track someone down on their days off. The burglary suspects were convicted and their paroles were revoked. Once again I was very proud of King and the way he performed in dealing with criminal suspects in extremely dangerous circumstances.

On December 8th, 1967 Anoka Police Sergeant Bill Foote spotted a vehicle driving in a radical manner in an Eastside neighborhood at 2:00a.m. As Sergeant Foote pulled this vehicle over, the passenger jumped out and ran off on foot. Turns out the vehicle was stolen in Minneapolis. Officer Joe Labonne, who was on patrol a few blocks away, noted the youth who ran from the vehicle ducking into an alley. Officer Labone contacted King and I by radio and advised us of his location. Upon our arrival I hooked King up to his thirty foot tracking leash and began an open area search of the area into the wind. King was trained in both open area search and tracking. In an open area search the dog searches for someone who may be in the immediate area by walking a pattern into the wind. This method of searching causes the dog to pick up a scent directly from wind blowing across a given area where a prey or suspect may be hiding. It is different from tracking where the dog takes the scent off the ground from a prey or suspect who has left the immediate area. As Officer Labonne had spotted the suspect in the immediate area, I believed he might still be close by, and an open area search was the quickest means to locate him if he was. We had only walked a few hundred feet when King picked up the scent and located the suspect hiding behind some residential trash cans. As we approached the trash cans King was huffing and puffing, low growling, and tugging on the leash. The suspect's spotted us, stood up and surrendered. They were placed under arrest for auto theft and taken into custody. Both suspects were under age 18, and held for the Minneapolis Police Department.

In his first year on the police department, King appeared at each elementary school, where I was able to talk about what he was trained to do, and why he was such an important asset to the force. I always talked about how Kings first job was to take care of me, by making sure that no bad guys tried to do anything to harm me, and that if they did he would be there to protect me. His secondary job was to make sure that no bad guys tried to harm the other officers he worked with, by being present at unruly crowd scenes, or searching buildings for suspects.

It is a well-accepted in law enforcement that the psychological effect of one police dog at a large crowd scene has the same impact as ten police officers. I always liked to explain to young people how a dogs scenting or smelling ability is so much more superior to that of humans, and how with all of our scientific knowledge we have not been able to come up with a machine that is better than a dogs nose.

After speaking to the young people about King's training and ability we usually would put on a demonstration of his obedience, and his ability to apprehend bad guys. King's favorite part was always after the demonstrations. He would be taken off his leash and allowed to roam amongst the children where he received their petting and affections. He was always affectionate toward them, and they were always affectionate toward him.

Eric and King

CHAPTER 7
RIOT IN THE COUNTY JAIL

On January 26, 1968, King and I had only been on duty working the dog watch for an hour. I received a radio call at 12:20a.m.directing me to return home as my wife Bonnie had called and said she may be having the baby. I returned home activating red lights and siren and Bonnie met me at the door. She was dressed and said her water had broken. I placed King in his kennel at home and had Bonnie get in the front seat of my squad car. I then went red lights and siren to Mercy Hospital, which was only about three miles from my house. I checked out at the hospital and told the dispatcher I didn't really know how long I would be. The dispatcher advised me that the supervisor had already called someone in to replace me, and that I was to remain at the hospital with my wife. The baby did not come quickly. Bonnie was in labor for about six hours before our son Eric was born. Fathers were not allowed at that time to be in the delivery room. I had to wait in an expectant father's waiting room until a nurse came and advised me of the birth. Then I had to wait even further until the baby was cleaned up and taken back to his mother before I could see them both. All I really remember is that it was a really trying time. Dr. Yelle came out later and advised me that both Bonnie and baby Eric came through everything fine and were doing well. When I finally got to see them Bonnie was very tired and the baby was sleeping. After two days in the hospital I got to take them both home.

On February 2nd, 1968, Police Chief Dave Hoagland announced the addition of a second police dog. For the past several months I had been working with Officer Ron Nicholas and his German Shepherd

Duke in all phases of police dog training. Duke turned out to be a dog with superior prey drive and almost a natural ability to master the training quickly. Chief Hoagland had determined that because of the increase in serious crimes we were experiencing in the city, and the value of having a police dog unit respond when appropriate, that there was a need for an additional dog. Officer Nicholas and I both worked the dog watch but we had different days off. The Chief's solution for getting the most K-9 Unit coverage was to alternate working our dog every other day and be present with the dog every day when the other officer was on days off. That did give us the most K-9 Unit coverage possible with two dogs and handlers.

POLICE GET ANOTHER DOG—Police Chief Dave Hoagland and Patrolman Ron Nicholas "inspect" Duke, a 65 pound German shepherd and the newest member of the Anoka Police Canine Corps. Duke's handler is Nicholas, who was trained under the supervision of Anoka Police Dog Handler Andy Revering, a graduate of the National Police Dog Academy of Kansas, where he was sent through the efforts of the Anoka Lions, Anoka Jaycees and American Legion Edward B. Cutter Post 102 of Anoka. Duke received the same training as King in obedience, criminal apprehension, tracking, searching, mob control and disarming. With the new addition, a police dog will be on duty at all times during late evening hours. Time spent by both men training this dog was done on their own time. Obtaining and raising the dog was at no cost to the city.

On March 15, 1968, King and I received a radio call that a citizen heard glass breaking in the rear of North Suburban Automotive on 5th Ave. South. Upon arrival we found a glass panel broken out of a rear overhead door. After another officer secured the front of the building, I yelled inside the broken out window, that we were the police and whoever was inside should come out with their hands up or we would be sending in a police dog. Hearing no response I sent King in through the panel that was broken out of the overhead door. I followed King in through the broken panel and as I observed King enter the office area of the building he went around behind a desk and I heard someone yelling, "Ouch! Ouch! Get him off me, get him off me." I immediately called King off and snapped on his leash. A young man came crawling out from under the desk, after which I had King watch him while I searched him. After turning the suspect over to other officers, we completed a search of the building and found no one else. The suspect was 18 years old and he was later returned to the Red Wing, Minnesota Training School for Boys, for burglary and violation of probation.

On May 31, 1968, at 6:15a.m. a radio broadcast went out to all Anoka Cars advising that the Elk River Police Department, which was located 10 miles West of Anoka, was chasing a stolen car at over 100 miles an hour on Highway 10 and headed toward Anoka. I placed my squad car cross ways on Highway 10 just East of 7th Ave. My vehicle was parked so that a driver wouldn't see it until it crested the hill on Highway 10. I got out of the car with King on a short leash with my left hand and grabbed my shotgun in my right hand. Officer Nicholas had stationed himself further down from where I was located on Highway 10. He had pulled his squad car off on the shoulder, left his red lights on, and got out with his shotgun. Within a few minutes the stolen vehicle being pursued crested the hill on Highway 10 and was headed right toward my vehicle. At the last second the driver turned to avoid crashing into my vehicle and was now headed straight toward King and me. As I was running to get out of the way of the vehicle with King in tow, I fired a round off from my shotgun at the windshield of the stolen vehicle. The pellets from my 12 gage round simply bounced off of the glass. As the vehicle continued toward Officer Nicholas he fired off three rounds from his shotgun at the vehicle. During this period of time police officers in Minnesota were authorized by law to use deadly force at fleeing felons. The vehicle veered off into the center median. The driver went across the median, up the other side of the freeway and was now driving the wrong way on the opposite lanes. He then drove up the down ramp and off the other side into the ditch. I got back into my vehicle after the car thief went by me and followed after the other squad cars which were in pursuit. When I learned the driver had bailed out of the vehicle after going into the ditch, I snapped on King's 30 foot tracking leash and started trailing him. We found the suspect in a barn where he was hiding, and turned him over to Elk River Officers. Turns out he was only 17 years old and was a recent release from the St. Cloud State Reformatory for Youth.

On June 9th, 1968, at 11:30p.m.King and I received a radio call to report to the Anoka County Jail and assist deputies with an unruly prisoner. Upon arrival at the jail King and I were buzzed in through the back door. As we entered the outer hallway of the jail I could hear a banging noise and someone yelling from inside the jail area. When I asked the deputy who buzzed us in to let King and me into the jail area to deal with the problem, he said the Lieutenant in charge did not want me to go in there. I asked the deputy for the name of the present Lieutenant in charge, he said it was Lieutenant Gleason and that he was on the phone with the Chief Deputy. When Lieutenant Gleason got off the phone I advised him that King and I had quelled unruly prisoners in the jail on several occasions and to let us into the jail area and we'll take care of the problem. He said he would not authorize that under the circumstances and the Chief Deputy was on the way down to the jail to deal with it. The banging noise and yelling from prisoners got louder in the jail area. When the Chief Deputy arrived I approached him about sending King and I into the jail area to deal with the problem as we had done several times in the past. The Chief Deputy was Ray Baker. I had known both him and Lieutenant Gleason since I became a police officer and felt they were both good leaders. Chief Baker advised me that the circum-stances inside the jail had escalated to the point where the prisoners were busting up sinks and toilet stools inside cells and throwing the pieces at deputies as they came in and tried to quell the situation. Chief Baker said he wanted me and King as well as Coon Rapids K-9 Officer Leroy Anderson and his dog Sarge to remain in the outer hallway and guard prisoners who would be brought out by deputies. A team of deputies put on helmets and protective body gear and went in with night sticks and mace and began arresting and dragging out prisoners who were rioting inside the jail area. They lined them up on the outer hall wall where King, Sarge and Officer Anderson and I guarded them until it was determined where they would be taken next. Due to the damage caused inside of the jail, Chief Baker had instructed that some of the prisoners would be taken to the Anoka City Jail and some others would be taken to the Hennepin County Jail. The prisoners caused several thousand dollars in damage to the Anoka County Jail during this riot and were eventually charged with Criminal Damage to Property and Rioting. As the jail remodeling was completed all of the ceramic glass sinks and toilet stools were replaced with the new steel type combination sinks and toilets. I always found it interesting that our city jail which was much smaller than the county jail and built before the present county jail was built yet it had steel walls, and steel sinks and toilets. My only assumption was when the present county jail was built they used ceramic sinks and toilets simply to save money at the time. That would not have surprised me as governments were sometimes guilty of opting for the lower bid versus safety. Anoka City Hall, the attached police facilities and jail were built by Federal Cartridge Corporation and donated to the city in the late 1950's. Federal Cartridge is a large manufacturing corporation in the City of Anoka, which appeared to have spared no expense in the construction of this facility, as it always appeared well built.

Federal Cartridge Corporation only had one request, they wanted the building designed in the shape of a handgun from the top. In the lobby of city hall, embedded in the floor, is a depiction of city hall located on the Rum River. It looks like a handgun and I was always impressed with that.

CHAPTER 8
POLICE DOG PROVES HERO IN CAPTURE OF GUNMAN

On Sunday, July 7, 1968, at 4:30a.m., I received a radio call from the Police Chief in Elk River requesting assistance with the police dog at a truck stop on the east end of their city, and about 10 miles from Anoka. The Chief advised that they were searching for an individual who had shot two people and fled into a field behind a truck stop. The Chief felt they had the field pretty well sealed off as the National Guard MP happened to be on a ride along with the State Patrol that weekend and they, along with other agencies had surrounded the field. I met Chief Earl Hohlen at the truck stop within ten minutes of receiving the call. The City of Elk River at this time, was only about 3000 residents and had five officers working full time, including the chief. By the time I got to the truck stop it was beginning to break day light. Chief Hohlen told me the man we were looking for had shot two individuals when they got in an argument over a bottle of whiskey. He said the suspect had a 22 caliber pistol and a 45 caliber automatic.

King Captures Gunman After Two Shootings

● King, the Rin-Tin-Tin of the Anoka Police Department, dragged a gunman from his hiding place in a swamp Saturday following the shooting of two rural Elk River men.

The youth, Thomas Nevin, 18, 1706 Queen ave. N., Minneapolis, was charged with careless use of a firearm in Sherburne county court Monday. He is being held in Anoka County Jail.

Elk River Police Chief Earl Hohlen received a call of a shooting about two miles e a s t of town. He notified the Sherburne C o u n ty Sheriff's office a n d requested the Anoka Police Department to send King. King and his handler, Patrolman Andy Rev-

King

ering arrived and Revering let King search the swamp area where Hohlen said he saw the suspect flee, leaving his car, which was stuck in the ditch. Police also apprehended a 16-year-old juvenile as he was riding in a tow truck he summoned to get the car out of the ditch. The youth was apparently with Nevin at the time of the shooting, but the Sherburne County Attorney has indicated there will be no charges brought against him.

King went into the brush ahead of Revering and Hohlen and a short time later, grabbed the suspect by the leg as he lay face down in the swamp grass. The suspect was apparently so startled he dropped the two loaded automatics he was holding and started yelling for help as King tugged him about 10 feet

from the dropped guns before Revering covered the suspect and ordered King to release him.

Hohlen said the shooting took place after an argument over a bottle of whiskey. The two who were shot were held by the other pair for about 15 minutes, Hohlen said.

Wounded were two cousins, Paul Hauan, 32, who was listed in serious condition at Mercy Hospital, with an abdominal wound, and Gerry Hauan, 21, who was treated and released at Mercy for a wound in the hand. Gerry drove himself and Paul to Mercy hospital after the shooting.

King, on July 25, is scheduled to receive the "Lassie Gold Award" on the "Clancy and Carmen" show at 7 a.m. on WCCO-TV.

He said the suspect had shot these two individuals with each of those guns. The Chief said his plan was for he and I to go into the field and use the dog for a decoy to draw the suspect's fire, and when that happened we would shoot him. I advised the Chief that we needed to move to the end of the field where the wind was blowing in our direction and then we would quarter the field so that the dog could use his nose to detect him. We grabbed our shotguns and went to the North side of this large grassy field. As we stepped from our vehicles into the field, I unsnapped King's leash and commanded him, "Find him, Find him boy." As King took off into the field, I hadn't realize that the grass was chest high on us and now we couldn't see where the dog was. I didn't want to call him back and give away our positions, nor did I want to call him off if he was onto the scent, so we just kept walking. We got about half way to the other side of the field when we heard the suspect yelling, "Get him off me, Ouch! Ouch! Get him off me." The next thing we saw was the grass breaking open in front of us and King was dragging the suspect out toward us by his leg. I called to King to release him as soon as I could observe he was not holding any weapons, and Chief Hohlen immediately went up and placed handcuffs on him. After turning the suspect over to other officers Chief Hohlen, King and I went back into the field to search for the suspects weapons.

King captures gunman who shot two people.

We found them a short distance from where King apprehended him. Both weapons were on the ground, one on top of the other, both hammers cocked and fully loaded. We learned later from the suspect that he was watching the Chief and me walking toward him in the field. He said he never saw the dog when King came up behind him and bit him in the back of the neck. He said it scared him so bad he dropped both guns. He said the dog then released his hold on his neck and grabbed him by a leg and began dragging him. As both victims eventually survived their bullet wounds, the suspect was charged with aggravated criminal assault. The producers of the Lassie television series picked up the story about this capture by King on the AP wire services after it appeared on the front page of the Minneapolis Sunday Paper. As a result they contacted the police chief in Anoka and advised him that they wanted to present King with the "Lassie Gold Award for Meritorious Action" on the "Clancy and Carmen" children's television show. Clancy and Carmen is a local Minneapolis/ St. Paul children's television show. Clancy is a television actor who portrays the role of a police officer and Carmen is a television actress who portrays the role of a nurse in this local television children's show.

On August 2nd, 1968, Sergeant Art Erickson went along with King and me to Minneapolis WCCO TV Studios to meet with Nurse Carmen of the Clancy and Carmen Children's Television Show to accept The Lassie Gold Award for Meritorious Action. The award was given to King by the producers of the Lassies Television Show for his efforts in the capture of a gunman who had shot two people and fled into a field.

It was a huge honor for King to have received this prestigious medal and he made all of us on the police department very proud.

Carmen the Nurse of the local television show "Clancy and Carmen" presents the Lassie Gold Award for Meritorious Action on behalf of the producers of the Lassie TV Show to King for capturing a gunman who had shot two people.

Toward the end of 1968 serious rioting began breaking out in major cities across the country. Some of the rioting was attributed to racial violence and others were related to the war in Vietnam. The

Watts Riots in Los Angeles, the Chicago Riots during the Democratic Convention and closer to home the Plymouth Avenue Riots in Minneapolis all led to a greater concern for public safety. In Anoka County under Mutual Aid Pacts city and county law enforcement agencies began training together to prepare for any local potential for rioting. King and I were directed by our agency to take part in mutual aid riot control training as a result of such actions. Captain John Hall of the Anoka Police Department coordinated the training every Wednesday for three hours. The training lasted six weeks. It was the kind of training King had never been exposed to before, but he took to it with ease and became quite aggressive when large numbers of angry crowds threatened him. It was all good training for King and would lead to his future effectiveness on a couple of occasions where he had to deal with a large number of aggressive

people. On a National level, as a result of the Federal Governments concern for the disasters which took place as a result of some of these riots, they passed legislation which provided funding for law enforcement officers to attend college. Apparently it was determined that the police were not educated enough which resulted in riots not being handled correctly, as least in some peoples view. An Omnibus Crime Control Bill was passed which among other things, created the Law Enforcement Assistance Program within the Justice Department to fund the college education of police officers. It was strictly voluntary of course, but I took advantage of it, along with several other police officers. I was a veteran besides, so this program caused me to be able to complete an AA Degree in Law Enforcement and a BA Degree in Criminal Justice Studies while working full time as a police officer. Between putting in the training required to Keep King at his peak performance and going to school part time, it kept me busy on my off time.

During the election in November of 1968, and as a direct result of the riots, a Minneapolis Police Detective by the name of Charles Stenvig, who was also the President of the Minneapolis Police Federation, got elected Mayor of Minneapolis. Mayor Stenvig sent a Minneapolis Police Officer by the name of Mike Fischer out to interview me about training dogs for the Minneapolis Police Department. I advised Mike that I would simply not have the time on a part time basis to train dogs for the Minneapolis Police Department. I further advised Mike that the Washington DC Metropolitan Police had one of the largest K-9 Units in the country, and that I was aware that they had a training program to assist other agencies. In fact I told Mike that they would provide the dog and the training at no cost as long as the agency sent an officer out and paid his board and room for twelve weeks. Mike took that proposal back to Mayor Stenvig. As a result the Minneapolis Police Department decided to send Officer Welton Copp out to Washington DC to train as their first K-9 Officer. In the middle of Officer Copps training Officer Fischer was sent to begin training with a 2nd class. When Officers Copp and Fischer returned from their training it was decided by the Minneapolis Police Department that they would train their own class of 8 more K-9 Officers. Officer Mike Fischer asked me if I would mind giving them a hand training this new class. I would work my normal shift from 11:00p.m. to 7:00a.m., sleep until noon, and get up and drive down to Minneapolis to help them for half a day training their new class. I'll never forget that first class graduation day. Mayor Stenvig handed completion certificates to each officer and his young son gave each dog a milk bone. Shortly thereafter Minneapolis Police applied for a federal grant under the Omnibus Crime Control Bill to build a new Police Dog Training Center. As a result they began training dogs for St. Paul and other Minnesota law enforcement agencies at no cost.

In early January of 1969 I began to take college evening classes at North Hennepin Community College on a regular basis. Classes usually began at 7:00p.m. and ended at 9:00p.m. That gave me enough time to get home and get ready for the dog watch shift I worked. The trouble was I needed a second car. Bonnie needed our family car to go to work and I couldn't use the take home police vehicle assigned to me to attend classes. The problem was solved when the two fellows who towed vehicles for the police department told me they had a vehicle they could sell me for $75.00. These two men worked for Main Motors Chevrolet/ Cadillac in Anoka and had the police towing contract. Vehicles that were towed and weren't claimed by owners ended up being the property of the towing company for the price of the tow. These two men told me they had a real nice 1962 Oldsmobile four door vehicle that was mechanically sound. They said the reason the price was so low was that someone had shot and killed themselves inside the vehicle and no one wanted to buy it. They had put new seat covers in the vehicle but it had kind of a lingering pungent scent inside the vehicle. I told them it would work for me as I just needed it for transportation back and forth to college. I put about three vehicle odor removal cards in the vehicle but my wife Bonnie would never get in that car. I also used it to haul King around to training whenever my squad was in for maintenance. My son never minded riding in it. I only kept that vehicle for a couple of years, before trading it for something else.

Eric & King

On January 7th, 1969, King and I were working the dog watch when at 11:40p.m. we received a radio call that a patient at the Anoka State Hospital had taken a female staff person at knife point out to her car and drove away, kidnapping her. A description of the vehicle followed and immediately thereafter Officer Ron Nicholas came on the radio and said he was behind the vehicle at 4th Ave. and the Pleasant Street Bridge headed west toward Ferry Street. Officer Nicholas's next radio transmission stated that the vehicle had turned left on Hwy # 10 and was now headed East on the Freeway. Just after the vehicle turned onto Hwy # 10 I came in behind Officer Nicholas's vehicle. I radioed to him that I would try to get in front of the suspect vehicle and we would try to box him in. As I was able to get in front of the suspect vehicle a Coon Rapids Police vehicle joined us at Hanson and Hwy # 10. As the Coon Rapids Officer came around to the left side of the suspect vehicle I began slowing down, and eventually came to a complete stop in front of the suspect vehicle. He initially slammed into the back of my vehicle and then tried to back up and slam into Officer Nicholas's vehicle. Officer Nicholas had already closed the gap when the suspect vehicle slammed into my vehicle and now the suspect could not move forward or backward. A second Coon Rapids Officer came up behind Officer Nicholas, jumped out of his vehicle at the same time I got out of my vehicle with King. The Coon Rapids Officer smashed out the window on the driver's side of the suspect vehicle, unlocked the door and grabbed the female staff member and pulled her from the vehicle and at the time I sent King into the vehicle. King grabbed hold of the suspect by the arm and dragged him out of the vehicle. The suspect was placed into custody and eventually booked for Kidnapping, Felony Assault, Auto Theft, and Resisting Arrest.

On January 16, 1969, while working the dog watch, King and I were called to assist the Anoka County Sheriff's Department who were searching for three youthful inmates who had escaped from the Minnesota Youth Treatment Center in Lino Lakes, Minnesota. Upon arrival we were advised that the Sheriff's Department surrounded wooded area behind the Youth Center. Two of the youth had already come out of the woods and surrendered to sheriff's deputies before I arrived. I shouted in a warning to the youth who was refusing to come out, I said, "I'm a police officer and I have a trained police dog, and if you don't come out in one minute with your hands up, I'm sending in the dog to find you. He will bite you." The youth yelled back to me. "Please don't send your dog I'm coming out." Shortly thereafter, the youth walked out to our location. He was taken into custody and returned to the youth center.

On February 22nd, 1969, at 12:30a.m. Sgt. Art Erickson discovered a break-in at the Cotton's Automotive Store on North Ferry Street.

King and I were called to search the building for suspects, but found no one inside. About an hour later we on patrol on West Highway # 10, and it was so foggy that I could barely see the center divider lines on the freeway. I had both back windows rolled halfway down as I normally did so that King could check both sides of the vehicle. I was traveling only a few miles per house when King began growling and pacing in the back seat. All of sudden I noticed someone walking quickly in front of me and crossing the freeway. I turned around and came back down the other side of the freeway. King began growling and pacing again when I noticed this man walking on the shoulder of the freeway. I pulled in behind him and turned on my red emergency lights. He stopped immediately when he heard King barking. I got out and shut the driver's door of my squad car. King jumped into the front seat and was hanging half way out the window as he was trained to do and was keeping a keen eye on the man in the fog. I noticed immediately as I approached this young man that his front pants pockets were bulging with what appeared to be a lot of coins. He was visibly having trouble keeping his trousers up due to the weight in his front pockets. I asked him where he got all the coins. He said he broke into a gas station. I placed him under arrest, put handcuffs on him and placed him in the front passenger's seat of my car. I advised him if he tried to escape or did anything to cause the dog to think he was going to attack me, that the dog would bite him. He sat very still in the front seat and King put his nose in the back of his neck and growled. Further investigation revealed that this suspect had broken into two service stations on West Highway # 10 and had also broken into Cotton's Automotive on Ferry Street. On February 24, 1969, Chief Dave Hoagland received a Letter of Commendation for King from Anoka County Attorney Robert W. Johnson. Mr. Johnson was a long time, highly respected County Attorney who eventually served as the President of the National District Attorney's and Juvenile Court Judge's Association. He wrote: "As you are well aware, we have today charged the above named person with Burglary. The unusual situation surrounding the apprehension of this individual leads me to send you this note of commendation in regard to the very effective way in which your dog King functioned. Certainly the evidence submitted to us supports the preposition that if the dog had not been with the officer, the defendant would not have been detected.

Beyond this matter of detection and apprehension of the defendant as I have mentioned above which certainly relates to the effective use of the dog, the case itself was well prepared, and I hope we are going to be able to effect a satisfactory conclusion to the case." Sincerely, Robert W. Johnson, Anoka County Attorney. The defendant eventually did serve time for all three burglaries. Robert W. Johnson was not only highly regarded in the legal community, but those in the law enforcement community, also thought of him as a person of integrity and a true professional in his field. For him to sit down and write a letter of commendation citing the very effectiveness of King in this case showed me that he truly recognized the value of police dogs in law enforcement, and I appreciated his comments.

On February 27th, 1969, King and I were asked to perform a police dog demonstration for Cub Scout Pack 318 at Lincoln Elementary School at 6:00p.m. This was one of many police dog demonstrations that King and I performed for Boys and Girl Scout Packs, as well as many other civic organizations. At this particular event we had dinner with the cub scouts and watched while they received awards. Then I got a chance to speak about King's value to the police department and the community. King would then demonstrate his abilities in basic obedience and apprehending bad guys. At end was always King's favorite part. I would take his leash off and he would go out to meet the cub scouts and receive their petting and praise. We usually went into each elementary school every year to demonstrate King's effectiveness, and he was always in high demand.

On March 7, 1969, about 1:00a.m. King and I received a call to a fight at the Clark Service Station on West Main Street. Upon arrival I observed three male young men pushing and swinging fists at each other. I got out of my vehicle, shut the front door and King jumped up to the front seat and hung half way out the window growling. As I approached all three individuals I told them they were all under arrest for disorderly conduct for fighting in public and that they were come along with me. Two of them began to walk with me back to my squad car, but the third one took a swing at me and said, "I won't be going with you." King, having observed what had taken place immediately jumped out the window, ran up to the aggressive individual and grabbed him by the arm. This young man quickly said, "Ouch, Ouch, call him off, I'll go with you." The other two gentlemen stood completely still with their mouths dropped open and didn't move as they watched King do his work. By this time another squad car arrived and all three individuals were taken into custody. All three of them were taken down and booked in the city jail where they eventually made bale and paid misdemeanor fines.

On September 19th, 1969, At 4:00a.m. King and I received a call in the Oakwood Drive area of Anoka. The dispatcher stated that a woman was home alone with her daughter and reports hearing someone trying to get in the front and back door of her home. Officer Mike Auspos responded to the call along with King and me. We arrived at the residence within two minutes and as Officer Auspos went to the front door to check on the occupants, I snapped on King's thirty foot tracking leash and he began to pull me around to the back of the house. King dove into a row of bushes in the back yard and was growling and snarling. A man immediately stood up and surrendered before King took hold of him. When I asked this man what he was doing behind this house, he said, "Waiting for you guys." The suspect had a Minneapolis address and appeared to be heavily intoxicated. We had earlier received a call of a car hung up on the center island and abandoned on the Freeway just East of Ferry Street. That vehicle registered to this same person. He was arrested for Public Intoxication and Vagrancy.

CHAPTER 9
KING TRIES TO SAVE NEWBORN BABY

On October 30, 1969, I was on my days off and at home when I heard King barking outside in his kennel. It was 2:30a.m. in the morning and I went to the back door turned on my yard light, didn't see anything, and told him to be quiet. I went back to bed when at 3:15a.m., I heard him barking again. I went to the back door, turned the yard light on again, and took notice that now it was lightly snowing. I didn't observe any sign of fresh tracks in the snow, and yelled at King again to be quiet, and returned to bed. At 4:20a.m. He was barking again. This time I got up, put on my trousers, shoes, and a jacket, went to the back door, turned on the yard light and walked out to King's kennel. It was still lightly snowing, but was fairly warm out. I again saw no sign of any tracks in the snow in my yard. I opened up King's kennel door, grabbed him by his choke chain, pulled on it and said sternly, "No, be quiet!" I walked back to the house and waited to see if he was going to bark again. I was no longer tired so I got cleaned up, dressed, and made some coffee. About 7:15a.m. there was a knock at my front door. When I opened the door there were three young elementary school age children from the neighborhood. They explained to me that they were on the way to school when they found a baby at the front steps of the Lutheran Church behind my home, and they wanted me to come with them.

King barks throughout
the night in effort to alert
someone about the baby.

Woman leaves newborn
baby in a laundry basket
at Church entrance.

I got a jacket on and we walked out through my back yard to the church. The Lutheran Church property was right up against my back yard. We walked to the front door of the church. At the front door of the church I observed another elementary school aged little girl from the neighborhood next to a cloths basket with a baby wrapped in a blanket. The baby looked to be new born, was alive, and seemed healthy. The basket was up under an overhang roof at the front door and was protected from the weather. I thanked the children for what they had done in locating the baby and picked the child up in the basket and took it back to my home to keep it warm. I called an ambulance to come and pick up the child to make sure it was ok, and then called child protective services to follow up on the investigation. The ambulance driver and his aid made a cursory check of the baby when they arrived and stated that the umbilical cord on the baby caused them to believe the infant was recently born. After the ambulance picked up the baby I took a huge milk bone out to King and told him he was a good boy for trying to tell me about the baby, and apologized for not listening to him. We learned later that a woman from the state hospital had the baby that evening on her own in a filling station bathroom and left it in the cloths basket at the front door of the church. It became quickly apparent that King had been trying to tell me all night that this baby had been left at the door step of the Church behind my property, and directly behind King's kennel. Thank God it was a fairly warm evening with light snow. My heart sinks when I think about that baby. If he had died I would have never have forgiven myself. I know now that God was trying to get a message to me that night through that big intelligent dog, and I wasn't listening. I always listened to him after that. The clear message in this story which had a very happy ending, is to always listen to your dog.

Bonnie, Eric, and King

On November 2, 1969, I asked my supervisor, Sgt. Art Erickson to help me build a small sled which could be pulled by King in the snow. My son Eric was almost three years old and I thought it would be something he would enjoy in the winter time. Eric played with and crawled all over King on a regular basis, but when King got tired of it he would go to the back door, sit in front of it, and wait for me to put him back out in his kennel. I thought the sled would help a little bit with their play time outside in the winter. Sgt. Erickson was a gifted carpenter and craftsman. He built a beautiful wooden box with steel skies and designed it so that it was just large enough for Eric to sit comfortably in it. The skies on the sled were solid steel on the back end. The front end had skies that were attached by two poles to King's harness and turned when he turned. It was a masterpiece, and even had King and Eric's name on the back of it. I had a shoe leather store make up a harness for King and trained him to pull the sled before placing Eric on it. It soon became popular for the smaller kids in my neighborhood to be pulled around in that sled by King and he seemed to never get tired of doing it.

On December 3rd, 1969, King and I were working the dog watch when at 2:15a.m. I received a radio call of a domestic at a home on North Ferry Street. The dispatcher reported that a woman called in and said her husband was going to kill her; and then the phone was hung up. The only other patrol car on duty was tied up on another call and we normally didn't respond to domestic calls alone. When I pulled up in front of the house I shut my vehicle lights off immediately and noted that there no lights on in the house. I had the windows down in my vehicle as I pulled up and I could hear a woman yelling, "He is going kill me, He is going kill me". And then it was silent. Under the circumstances I felt I need to respond. I went to the front door with King on a short leash. Even though it was winter, the screen door was closed, but the inner door was open. I could not hear anyone inside. I knew if I sent King inside, he would only go after the person who was being aggressive. I didn't say anything, I just opened the door and sent King in. When I didn't hear any sounds for about a minute I stepped inside. The house was totally dark. When I shined my flashlight into the living room I observed a middle aged gentleman standing facing me with a handgun pointed at me. King was sitting directly in front of him and not moving or making a sound. The man said to me, "Get that son of a bitch out of my living room, or I'll shoot him." I walked up snapped my short leash on King and backed up two paces. I told the gentleman that we could not leave and I needed to know where his wife was.

King disarms Domestic Violence suspect who
was threatening to kill his wife.

He said, "I don't know where the hell she is, but if you don't get out of my house someone is going to get hurt." About that time Anoka County Deputy Sheriff Bob Drowns came into the room behind me and moved to my left. Deputy Drowns began a conversation with the gentleman to the point where I felt he had him sufficiently distracted that I could move to disarm him. I inched closer to him as Deputy Drowns continued to keep his attention. Finally, I dropped King's leash and grabbed his right hand which had the handgun and pushed him up against wall. At the same time King jumped in and grabbed him on the inside of his right leg. In the same movement I pulled out my own handgun with the full intention hitting this man in the head to further gain control. He was a large man. As I pulled out my gun I noted that he came up with his left hand in which he held a knife. So now with my left hand I'm pushing his right gun hand against the wall and with my gun in my right hand I'm pushing his left hand which is holding onto a knife also against the wall, and King is still biting him on the leg. About this time another Deputy Sheriff arrived and began spraying tear gas over my right shoulder into the man's face. The tear gas of course came back and hit me in the face. Also about this time Officer Rudy Betlach arrived from my own department. Officer Betlach grabbed King's leash and attempted to control the dog. King turned around and bit him. At this point I just said, "Someone take the gun and knife out of his hands." Both Deputy Sheriff's took care of that and placed him in custody. The judge eventually sentenced this man to 30days in jail. Several months later I had stopped into an all-night restaurant in my community for breakfast. I was sitting at the counter when this gentleman I encountered in this domestic came in and sat next to me at the counter. He wanted to tell me that King had taught him a hard lesson. He said he finally divorced his wife, and went to Alcoholics Anonymous and is getting his life back together. He thanked me and wished me well.

On January 29, 1970 while working the dog watch at 3:15a.m. Officer Mike Auspos was checking out a van parked on State Ave. near Main Street. As Officer Auspos approached the vehicle, one man opened the passenger door and ran from the scene. Officer Auspos found a box containing drug paraphernalia near the van and arrested the driver. King and I were contacted by radio and advised to respond to the scene and begin a search for the man who ran from the scene.

Upon arrival, I snapped on King's thirty foot leash and inserted him into the passenger's side of the vehicle to obtain a scent. He picked the scent up quickly and took off trotting at a fast pace pulling me along behind. We went for about three blocks when he turned, went up the driveway to a house on Branch Street, and went to the back door. I knocked on the door and a woman answered the door. I explained to her what had taken place and that my dog had tracked someone to this house. She said her and her children had been sleeping inside but that we were invited to go ahead and search the home. King entered the back door, went immediately to the basement doorway and down the stairs. He started to go into an open door to the basement bathroom when the door was slammed in his face. I yelled to the person inside, "This is the police and I have a trained police dog. If you don't come out in two minutes with your hands up I'm kicking in the door and sending in the dog." The person inside shouted back, "Please don't send him in, I'm coming out, I give up." As a result of a follow-up investigation we learned that the driver of the van lived at this location and the suspect who ran into the house was a friend of his. Both were charged with possession of drug paraphernalia. They ended up serving 90day and 60 day jail sentences.

On March 1st, 1970, King and I were working the dog watch when at 1:30a.m. King and I received a radio call to proceed to Larry's Laundromat where two girls reportedly had been assaulted. Upon arrival I learned that the girls were in the Laundromat doing laundry when three young men came in who appeared to them to have been drinking. Words were exchanged and two of the young men ended up striking the two girls. The girls showed me the direction that they said these men took off walking. I put King's thirty foot leash on and gave him the command, "Find them, Find them Boy." He immediately put his nose to the ground and took off tugging hard on the leash. We went down several different blocks for about one mile when we ran onto three young men walking together who fit the descriptions given by the girls. The young men all turned around to face us when they heard King coming up fast, huffing and puffing and pulling on his leash. I told them, "I'm a police officer, remain where you are now, and don't try to run from me, as I have a trained police dog." They all remained completely still. I approached the three of them King began growling lowly. Two of the young men immediately said they were sorry for what they had done before I had even accused them of anything. I radioed for another car come and pick them up as I had arrested them for minor consumption and disorderly conduct. All of them were juveniles.

On March 25th, 1971, Captain John Hall advised me that King and I were to accompany him down to the Minneapolis/St. Paul German Shepherd Club. He said the club wanted to honor King for police service over the past couple of years. When we arrived for this ceremony, several members of the Minneapolis/St. Paul German Shepherd Club were in attendance. Captain Hall spoke of King's effectiveness in apprehending criminal suspects since he came onto the police department in 1967.

DOG CLUB HONORS POLICE DOG—The German Shepherd Dog Club of Minneapolis-St. Paul on Thursday presented a plaque for community service to the Anoka Police Department and Police Dog King. Capt. John Hall spoke to the group and King. Patrolman Andy Revering, King's handler, and Patrolman Al Campbell gave a demonstration. The presentation was made in the Twin Cities Obedience Training Club at 807 13th Ave. S., Minneapolis. Above are Capt. Hall, Revering, King and Jackie and Tom McIntyre of the Dog Club.

King is made honorary member and cited for Meritorious Service by the Minneapolis/St. Paul German Shepherd Club

King and I gave a short demonstration after Captain Hall was done speaking. Finally, the German Shepherd Club gave King a plaque which had a beautiful German Shepherd's head in gold as a background and a gold plate which read, "Presented to KING Anoka Police Dog for Meritorious Service to His Community—March 25, 1971 G.S.D.C. Mpls-St. Paul." Once again I was very proud of that Old Dog.

On May 15, 1970 King and I were working the dog watch when we received a radio call at 2:00a.m. to see a woman at a home on 7th Ave. South. Upon arrival I was advised that the woman had just returned home from her job at Federal Cartridge Company and when she went to check on her ten year old daughter in her bedroom she was gone. She woke up her husband and he said their daughter went to bed at 9:00p.m. One of the girl's friends who was contacted by the mother said she had seen the girl earlier in the evening in George Greene Park. George Greene Park was about three hundred yards from the girl's home. I obtained a piece of recently worn clothing of the girl's from the mother. When I snapped on King's thirty foot tracking leash and let him take a sniff of the clothing he immediately charged off toward George Greene Park. King didn't have his nose on the ground, but was sniffing high in the air and appeared to be taking the scent directly from the wind blowing in our direction. As we crossed into the park and got close to the swimming pool area he headed straight for a park bench. On the park bench King found the little girl wrapped in a blanket, still in her pajamas and clutching two dolls. She was sound asleep. As King got closer to her he stuck his nose under the blanket and licked the little girl across the cheek, which startled her and woke her up. She smiled and gave King a big hug. When I asked her what she was doing in the park instead of being home in bed. She said, "My mom and I got into an argument tonight before she went to work, and I just wanted to worry her a little bit." I told her, "You have worried both your parents a lot, don't ever do it again," and took her home. Her mom and dad were so glad to see her when she was returned home that they just wanted to hug her and didn't seem much concerned about disciplining her for her conduct. I believed the girl came from a good family, so I just lectured her a bit before returning to duty.

CHAPTER 10
FBI PRAISES POLICE DOG PROGRAM

On August 29th, 1971, Captain John Hall advised me that Richard G. Held, the Special Agent in Charge of the Minneapolis FBI approached him about Anoka's K-9 Unit being guests of the FBI, and attending the North Dakota Peace Officers Association Annual Conference in September. The FBI was proposing that Captain Hall, King, and I attend the conference to demonstrate the effectiveness of police dogs.

FBI Lauds Police Dog Demonstration

The Federal Bureau of Investigation and the Bismarck, North Dakota Police Department today commended the Anoka Police Department Canine Corps for conducting the police dog demonstration during the North Dakota Peace Officers Association 60th annual conference Sept. 8-10.

Anoka sent Capt. John Hall and Patrolman Andy Revering with Police Dog King to the conference at the request of the FBI.

Richard G. Held, Special Agent in Charge, told Police Chief Dave Hougland that the three Anoka representatives "did an outstanding job in conducting the police dog demonstration and added considerably to the success of the overall conference. "In my opinion, their presence was by far the highlight of the meeting."

The conference was held in Bismarck and was attended by over 300 lawmen and was conducted with the assistance of the FBI.

Captain Hall explained to me that it was a huge honor to be invited by the FBI to make this presentation on their behalf, and was clear they felt police dogs had a place in law enforcement. I knew that Captain Hall was a Graduate of the FBI National Academy and had an excellent working relationship with the local FBI. The FBI National Academy is a three month long Police Management Training Program totally sponsored by the FBI for local police administrators and taught at their facilities in Washington D.C. Although I knew little about the FBI National Academy at the time, I was privileged to attend it myself later on in my law enforcement career. In 1971 J. Edgar Hoover was the Director of the FBI. Mr. Hoover became the Director at age 24 when it was a small fledgling investigative body of the Justice Department. He has led the FBI for over 40 years and built it into the premier law enforcement agency in the world. He was well known for expecting a high degree of professionalism from his agents and was considered to be a tough disciplinarian. One of the responsibilities of the FBI was to provide training to local law enforcement. When we arrived in Bismarck, North Dakota an FBI agent was with Captain Hall and me every moment. I got the impression they wanted to make sure we didn't do anything to make them look bad. Under Hoover's reign if an agent was responsible for embarrassing the FBI he could end of stationed in Omaha. Our demonstration at the North Dakota Peace Officer's Conference went really well. Captain Hall spoke first and talked about the cases King and I had been involved with. I spoke next and talked about the dogs training and how that related to police work. We then performed a demonstration of the dog's effectiveness. Special Agent in Charge Richard Held, of the Minneapolis Office of the FBI thanked us and praised us highly for our performance, contending that we were the highlight of the conference. It was truly an honor to receive such high praise from the FBI, who were generally held in high regard by the law enforcement community during this period. King and I both enjoyed taking part in this conference and it was something I wouldn't soon forget.

On November 15th, 1971 King and I were working the dog watch when at 1:35a.m. we received a radio call of a silent alarm at the East Main Medical Clinic located at Main Street and 9th Ave. Officer Ron Sharbonno had also responded to call. Upon arrival we noted a broken window on the front side and West end of the building. The doors were locked so we could not obtain entry. Officer Sharbonno put in a call for someone from the East Main Clinic come down with a key so that we didn't have to break down a door to check it out. One of the doctors arrived and let us in the building. We searched and secured the building, but King kept going toward a locked door to a surgery room on the West side of the building where the broken window appeared to be. The doctor on the scene said that door was never locked and he said he would search the front desk for the key. As he went up to the front desk I yelled out, "If there is anyone inside, you better come out now with your hands in the air as I have a police dog and will send him in." A voice from inside yelled back, "Go ahead and send him I've got a gun". Hearing the individual inside say he had gun, Officer Sharbonno pointed his 357 Magnum at the door knob, pulled the trigger and blew the door open. I sent King inside and he grabbed hold of the suspect by arm who was holding a scalpel. As King bit down harder on the suspects arm he dropped the scalpel. When I could see that he did not have a gun I called King off of him. I took the suspect out to my vehicle and placed him in my vehicle. My new K-9 vehicle had a prisoner storage compartment right behind where King's area was behind the front seat. We learned later the suspect was a drug addict and broke into the surgery room and was drinking Novocain. On the way to the county jail King barked at the prisoner who was separated from him by a metal screen in the prisoner compartment. As King had gotten older, it seemed like every time he barked in a confined space he would pass gas. I kept telling King to knock it off, as it appeared he was gassing the prisoner all the way to jail. Turns out when we got to the jail I was wrong about King. It wasn't him that was causing the stench. The prisoner apparently got so frightened when King came in the surgery room and apprehended him that he had a bowl movement in his trousers. I'm sure the fact that he was drinking Novocain didn't help prevent that problem.

On December 3rd, 1971, King and I were working the dog watch when at 2:15a.m. I received a radio call to assist the Plymouth Police Department in Hennepin County. Plymouth Police surprised two suspects burglarizing a church. The pair were also suspects earlier in an armed robbery in Golden Valley. Plymouth and Golden Valley Police had chased the two suspects into a wooded area and were requesting King and me to help locate them. We arrived on the scene and I snapped on King's thirty foot leash. I put King in the area where the two suspects were last seen entering the woods. King started out a little slow, but then he seemed to hit the scent and began tugging hard on the leash. Three Plymouth Police Officers followed along behind us as we continued on the trail. The trail took us about seven miles when we observed the two suspects in an open clearing ahead. They began to run from us, but as King closed in, they both surrendered. Plymouth Officers eventually took them into custody.

On December 23, 1971, my wife Bonnie announced to me that she was pregnant again and we were going to have another baby. We had talked about having another child a few months ago so this was good news for both of us. Bonnie also told me that her doctor had advised her that the rules changed regarding expectant fathers and that now I could be present in the delivery room when the child was born. I was truly excited to hear about that. I didn't think there could be anything more special than being present at the birth of your own children. That wasn't possible when my son Eric was born, so I was really looking forward to being there when the new baby arrived. To me it would be like watching a miracle take place.

On January 1st, 1972, King and I were working the dog watch on New Year's Eve when at 12:30a.m. I received a radio call to assist the Hennepin County Sheriff's Department at Heggie's Pizza in Champlin, Minnesota, just across the Mississippi River from Anoka. Deputies were attempting to serve a warrant and receiving resistance from a large mob. When King and I pulled into the parking lot I observed a Hennepin County Sheriff's marked vehicle parked directly in front Heggie's Pizza. A Deputy had a hold of a man by the arm on the ground and a large crowd was attempting to pull him away from the deputy by his leg. A second Deputy was attempting to control the crowd, but was being physically pushed around by other members of the crowd. When I got out of my vehicle, King got out with me and I sent him directly into the crowd. He grabbed hold of the first person who had a hold of the Deputy's prisoner by the arm and pulled him to the ground. Then he let go of that person and went directly back at the crowd growling and barking at them. They immediately dispersed. We took three people into custody as well as the person the Deputies had the warrant on. This was a great example of King's crowd control training from 1968 coming to full fruition. When King went after that crowd, their eyes all got huge, and they all turned and ran to get out of his way. Now I know where that old saying comes from, of one police dog being as effective as ten police officers.

On June 6, 1972, King and I were working the dog watch when at 1:15a.m I received a radio call to assist the Anoka County Sheriff's Department with a noisy field party involving "Hell's Angels" about three miles north of the City of Anoka off of Hwy # 47. As I approached the area where the party was reported to be taking place I noticed a lot of light off of Hwy # 47 in a large field. I slowed and found a dirt road that led into the party area. I was about a half mile off of Hwy # 47 on this dirt road when I came upon three individuals with "Hell's Angels" jackets blocking the roadway with a vehicle and standing guard. One of these individuals, whom I recognized, walked up to me and asked what I wanted. "I told him that this field was private property and we had a report that a loud party was taking place." While we were speaking, King had his head out the window of my police vehicle, which was rolled half way down, and growling and barking at this individual. This gentleman said to me, "Andy, I think I can pet your dog." I said, "Well, I don't think you can, but if you feel like you must, go ahead and try." He immediately reached up toward King's head. The big dog grabbed him by his leather coat sleeve and dragged him halfway into the vehicle. He said, "Ok, Ouch, Ouch, I guess I can't pet him." I called King off, and he fell onto the ground. I helped him get up and said to him, "What do you think about breaking up this party?" He said, "Fine, I'll get them all outta here, right away." Ten minutes later they were all gone, and five minutes after that the Sheriff's Deputies showed up. Deputy Anderson said, "So, where's this big party." I told him, "Not to worry, King took care of that quite efficiently."

On August 18, 1972, King and I were working the dog watch when at 3:16a.m. we received a radio call of a silent alarm going off at the Rapid Sports Center which is in the City of Coon Rapids right on Anoka/ Coon Rapids City boundary on Coon Rapids Blvd. Anoka Officer Ron Sharbonno was very close to this location and responded to assist Coon Rapids Police. Officer Sharbonno was the first officer to arrive on the scene, and as he pulled into the parking lot a pick-up truck raced out. Officer Sharbonno took up the chase east on Coon Rapids Blvd. The pick-up went about two miles before it skidded into a ditch and two people got out and fled into a wooded area of the City of Coon Rapids. A Coon Rapids Officer radioed for King and me and requested we come to the scene of the crashed pick-up and see if we could pick up a trail. We arrived within two minutes and I snapped on King's thirty foot tracking leash. I had King jump into the cab of the suspect pick-up. He sniffed around on the seat and took off South into the woods toward the Mississippi River. As we exited a wooded area and headed out into large open tall grassy area King's head came up and I could tell he was close to his prey. He proceeded a few more feet and jumped into the tall grass and grabbed hold of one of the suspects by his leg. I could hear this person yell, "Ouch, Ouch, Ouch, call off your dog, I give up." I immediately called King off and the suspect stood up quickly with his hands in the air. He soon gave us the name of his accomplice, who was later apprehended. The suspect that King apprehended was charged with burglary and was found to already be on Probation from Morrison County, Minnesota.

On August 31st, 1972, King and I had only reported for duty on the dog watch, and were still at the office when I received a phone call from Bonnie who said to me, "I think my water just broke and its time." I told her I'd be right home. I raced home red lights and siren, and placed King in his kennel. Bonnie was waiting at the door when I arrived. I placed her in the front seat of my squad car and raced again, red lights and siren to the hospital. When we got to the hospital a nurse told us that it looked like this was going to happen quickly. Unlike when our son Eric was born, which took hours, our daughter Stephanie arrived on the scene within the first hour. I was all decked out in a gown, mask, and gloves, and was holding Bonnie's hand when it happened. It was and still is the most beautiful event that I have ever witnessed. It truly was like witnessing a miracle. There is no other way to describe it. We were both very happy. I couldn't wait to introduce Eric to his new sister. King had already been through this before when Eric came along, so I knew he would have no problem with the new baby.

Andy's daughter Stephanie & King

On September 8, 1972, King and I were working the dog watch when at 11:50p.m. I received a radio call from a Coon Rapids Officer requesting King and I assist them with a large beer party in the woods off Hanson Blvd. and Highway 242. Upon arrival King and I, along with eight Coon Rapids Police Officers, and a couple of deputy sheriffs moved in on a crowd of 24 teenage youths. As a Coon Rapids Police Sergeant announced to the group that they were all under arrest for minor consumption and disorderly conduct, and how they were going to be transported to the Coon Rapids Police Department for processing, King growled and barked at them on the end of his leash to make sure they understood. We had no difficulties with any of these young people as they were transported, processed, and released to their parents.

In October of 1972, King and I spent several days at the Anoka County Fair Grounds assisting in training Officer Jack Richardson and his dog Baron from the Champlin, Minnesota Police Department, and Craig Gorsuch, and his dog Ivan with the Coon Rapids, Minnesota Police Department. Officer Leroy Anderson and his dog Sarge of the Coon Rapids Police Department, who trained with me earlier, was also present during these training exercises.

On December 30, 1972, Chief Dave Hoagland appointed me to a detective position and asked me to place King on sort of semi-retirement at my home. The Chief had already selected Anoka Officer Al Campbell to attend the next Minneapolis Police Dog School in the spring, but he wanted King to remain on stand-by duty if he was needed. King by this time was nine years old. Most police dogs having a working life of about seven to eight years. German Shepherds had a tendency to end up with hip dysplasia at eight to ten years old. King was already afflicted with dysplasia and had lost a lot of strength in his back legs. I advised the Chief that I was sure we could continue to use King on a stand-by basis until Officer Campbell graduated from Police Dog School.

On February 1st, 1973, Chief Hoagland had become even more concerned that we only had a police dog on stand-by duty because of an increase in serious crimes and assaults on police officers. He advised me that he would very much like to put King back to work full time until Officer Campbell graduated from police dog school and was able to return to work. The Chief further advised me that he wished for me to remain at my duties as a detective and wanted to know if I thought King could be worked with another officer. I advised the Chief that because King loved to go to work, and he got along with all of the Anoka Officers I felt comfortable that he could go to work with another officer. The Chief wanted to know what I thought of assigning King to Officer Dennis Reihe. Officer Reihe was a seasoned officer who worked on my shift when I worked King and he got along really well with the dog. He was also a former Air Force Air Policeman so in my view he had a solid background. I advised the Chief that I felt I only needed to spend a week or so working with King and Officer Reihe to bring them up to speed and they should work out just fine. He agreed, approved the arrangement and told me to go ahead and set it up. Officer Reihe didn't have kennel facilities at his home, and this was only a temporary assignment until Officer Campbell returned from police dog school, so he agreed to pick King up at my house when he came on duty and would drop him off at the end of his shift. I spent about a week with Officer Reihe and King going over the training and allowing them to bond. I made sure I advised Officer Reihe that the most important thing to do as a dog handler was to listen to your dog. They began their duties as a team and worked very effectively together.

On July 20th, 1973, Officer Al Campbell and his dog Major graduated from the Minneapolis Police Department's Police Dog School. I had found Major as a German shepherd pup when he was in the City of Anoka Dog Pound and adopted him. I had raised him for the purpose of eventually replacing King, when the old dog couldn't work anymore. After donating Major to the police department to attend dog school with Officer Campbell the Chief said to me, "I like the fact that his name is Major and he will outrank the two Captains on the police department. I'll be curious as to what they think of that." The Chief had a good sense of humor. Officer Campbell and Major began their duties on the dog watch. The Chief advised Officer Reihe that he still wanted him to work King when Officer Campbell was on his days off. The work schedules were worked out to assure the Chief's orders were carried out.

On July 28, 1973, Sergeant Russ Rollins retired from the police department after twenty years of service. Within a couple weeks of Sergeant Rollin's retirement the police department performed written and oral board examinations of all police officer candidates who were eligible to replace him. I was one of those candidates. When all of the testing was completed Chief Hoagland advised me that I had come out number one of all the candidates and that he would be appointing me the new Sergeant effective on August 23, 1973.

As the new Sergeant on the police department I was assigned to supervise the officers on the dog watch. It was the same shift I worked as a dog handler. Not only was I responsible for supervising the officers on dog watch but I was also assigned responsibility of overseeing the training and readiness of the police dog unit. I was only a detective for about one year and enjoyed the follow up investigations that detectives were responsible for, but enjoyed police work in the field much more.

CHAPTER 11
POLICE DOG KING RETIRES

On March 1, 1974, Chief Hoagland announced the retirement of Anoka Police Dog King. The Chief said, "The ownership of Anoka Police Dog King has been transferred to Sgt. Andy Revering. King is now completely retired from active and standby duty with the police department." A local newspaper article written about King upon his retirement stated: King came to work for the department in Feb., 1967. He was the first police dog to be used successfully over a continuous period in the metropolitan area and is recognized as the dog responsible for bringing on police dogs back to use in this area. Over the years, King has been responsible for numerous arrests and has been cited for some of his captures by local authorities and by the producers of the Lassie show, the American Federation of Police, and the Minneapolis St. Paul German Shepherd Club. King is now nine years old and will live out the remainder of his years at the home of Sgt. Revering. King has been replaced by Major, a young German Shepherd which was raised by Revering and is handled by Patrolman Allan Campbell."

Police Dog King Retires

3-7-74

The ownership of Anoka Police Dog King has been given to his first handler, Sgt. Andy Revering. King is now completely retired from active and standby duty with the police department.

King came to work for the department in Feb., 1967. He was the first police dog to be used successfully over a continuous period in the metropolitan area and is recognized as the dog responsible for bringing police dogs back into use in this area.

Over the years, King has been responsible for numerous arrests and has been cited for some of his captures by local authorities and by the producers of the Lassie show, the American Federation of Police and the Minneapolis-St. Paul German Shepherd Club.

King is nine years old and will live out the remainder of his years at the home of Revering. King has been replaced by Major, a young German Shepherd which was raised by Revering and is handled by Patrolman Allan Campbell.

KING - with Sgt. Andy Revering's six-year-old son Eric.

When King retired he was actually closer to nine and one half years old. His dog house was built with a separate extra wall, so that when he entered it he could go into the inner room and get completely out of the wind. German shepherds have a double coat and can survive in just about any kind of weather. As King got older I knew that he would suffer the effects of hip dysplasia and arthritis and keeping a dog warm is important when they are older, especially in the winters of Minnesota. As a result a couple years earlier I attached King's dog house to my garage, which was heated. King had the ability to go into his dog house and walk through to a heated and comfortable area just for him. He didn't seem to care for that warm dog house I created for him all that much. He was a long haired German shepherd and liked to spend most of his time outside. I had a strong feeling that King was going downhill fairly fast and suspected he may pass away sometime during the coming winter months. I knew that if he passed away during the winter I wouldn't be able to bury him properly, simply because the ground would be to frozen to dig a grave for him. I decided to dig a grave this summer, while the ground was still soft behind my garage, and cover it with a large piece of plywood. I also stacked some wood on top of the plywood so that the area didn't get disturbed.

Each day that I went to work on the dog watch, I always walked out to King's kennel to pet him and tell him goodbye when I left for my shift. Like every police dog, King lived to go work. When he couldn't do that anymore he started to indicate signs of depression. His head was usually down and he had a pretty sorrowful look in his eyes.

On February 2nd, 1975, at 10:15p.m. I went out to King's kennel before leaving for work to pet him and tell him goodbye. He appeared extremely slow when he came to greet me. I petted him, scratched his neck and told him I had to go to work now, but I'd see him in the morning. When I returned from work at 7:45a.m. on the morning of February 3rd, 1975 it had begun to snow lightly. I walked from my car to King's kennel. I didn't immediately see him come out of his dog house to greet me. As I approached his kennel I called his name, but then I saw him. He was lying down, outside of his dog house, and half covered with snow. I knew before I opened his kennel door and checked him that he was gone. This is when grown men cry. I could feel it welling up inside me as I picked him up to carry him behind the garage. As I laid him down next to the grave site that I prepared for him, I felt the cold tears running down my face in the winters cold. I sat down in the snow covered ground with his big head on my lap. I told him how much I appreciated him being my partner these past few years, thanked him for being my friend and saving my life more than once. I'm not sure how long I sat with him before I covered him with a blanket, placed him the gravesite, and covered it with frozen dirt. I'm not sure how long I was outside taking care of King and saying my goodbyes. When I finally went into the house, Bonnie met me at the door. I forgot that it was Saturday and she would be home from work. She said to me, "Where have you been? I saw your car in the drive way." The kids were still in bed so I told her about King. She began to cry and we just held each other for a few seconds. I knew that Bonnie loved that dog as much as I did. She was there when I first came home with him and knew about everything we had been through. I told Bonnie I needed to tell Eric about his passing. I use to take Eric along on training exercises with me and King ever since he was above five years old. He was also the one King use to pull around in that sled we had made for the two of them. Eric was also close to the old dog. When Eric got up I took him downstairs to my home office in the basement. He was now eight years old. I sat him down and shut the door. I had already told Eric how long German Shepherds live and what happens to them as they get older. When I began to tell him about coming home this morning and finding King covered in snow in his kennel, he began to cry. I held him for a little bit and then we both went out to his gravesite behind the garage and just stood there for a bit. We walked back to the house where Bonnie was preparing breakfast and all sat down together. We didn't speak of King after that, for at least a few days.

After I had made Sergeant Chief Hoagland advised me that he was putting my name in to attend the FBI National Academy in Washington DC. The FBI National Academy was a three month long police management school which was sponsored by the FBI. The FBI Academy was divided up between attendees who wanted to become FBI Agents, and attendees who were police supervisor's taking police administration and management courses. I had volunteered to attend early if someone backed out of one the classes before I was scheduled to attend. Someone did back out and I began attending the 101st Session of the FBI National Academy on June 1st, 1975. Besides classroom training, all attendees took part in physical fitness training, and firearms training. On one of my first visits to the Library at the Academy I became acquainted with a young man working in the library. This young man was waiting to get into a new FBI Agents class and got this temporary job working in the library. He actually confronted me when I came into the library and told me that he had read a couple of articles I written on police dogs in a couple of police journals. He said he had looked up the names of people attending the present FBI National Academy class and knew that I was going be in attendance. He said he recognized me from a picture in one of my articles. He told me he had two white German shepherds that he couldn't do anything with and wanted to know if I could give him some tips. I told him," I'm going to be here for three months, so why don't you bring the dogs out to the academy on weekends and I'll help you train them." I told him to get good choke chains and leather leashes for both dogs. We began training the dogs on weekends at the Academy. The owner of the dogs primarily wanted to teach both dogs basic obedience, but wanted also to ensure they would be protective if they needed to be. In one of my classes at the Academy and FBI Agent who was involved in Hostage Negotiations and Hostage Rescue spoke to us. FBI Tactical Teams around the country were developing training in this area and seemed to be acceptable to new ideas. I proposed to this instructor that police dogs should be part of any tactical team response and could be used as decoys so that law enforcement snipers could perform their task. He wanted to know how I could demonstrate that. I told him I was helping a young man who worked in the library train his German Shepherds on the week end and if he wanted to come out and watch I'd show him how it worked. We had done enough training with the dogs in their protection work that I felt confident we could perform a bold demonstration. Not only did the FBI instructor show up, but he brought along an FBI photographer with him.

I had asked a female member of my class to volunteer to be our victim in the demonstration. The females name was Carol Daily. She was a detective with the Sacramento County Sheriff's Department. Detective Daily would become the Lead Investigator in the famous Golden State Killer Case. Her husband was a Sergeant with the same organization. We went about setting up various scenarios where Detective Daily was the hostage and I was the armed hostage taker. I told the young dog handler not be concerned because the dog would only come after me when he sent him. The dogs know the difference between who is an aggressor and who is an innocent victim. The FBI Academy even had an old airplane permanently set up in their training area that we used to stage hostage situations and how the dog would come into play. Today police dog teams are a regular part of swat teams and used in every day tactical exercises.

While attending the FBI National Academy in 1975 Andy Revering plays the bad guy while Sacramento County Detective Carol Daly plays the hostage, in a demonstration of K9's assisting in hostage rescue.

I was about half way through my training at the FBI Academy when I walked into a law class. It was unusual to see the Director of Training for the FBI National Academy in our class, and everyone was curious as to what it was all about. Before the class got started that morning, the Director got up and read from a letter he had received. The letter as read by the Director was sent to him by my police chief. It read, Dear Mr. Director, please advise Sergeant Andrew C. Revering of the Anoka, Minnesota Police Department that Captain John Hall has retired, and I am appointing Sergeant Revering to replace him as Captain, and it was signed Chief Dave Hoagland, Anoka, Minnesota Police Department. All fifty of my classmates in the room applauded when the director was done reading the letter. The Director asked me to come up. He shook my hand, congratulated me and gave me a copy of the letter.

After graduating from the FBI National Academy and returning to my agency, Chief Hoagland advised me that I would be the Captain in charge of the uniform division of the police department.

On July 16, 1976, I made a presentation to the Anoka City Council on behalf of the Anoka Police Federation (the fraternal arm of the police department), Anoka Jaycees, Anoka Lions Club, and the Anoka American Legion Club. The last three clubs were the original sponsors to purchase King. The proposal was to name a small neighborhood children's city park at Park Street and Porter Ave. after Anoka's first Police Dog and to place a statue of King in the park. The park would be called "King Memorial Park." The proposal was requesting that the city build the brick base for the statue which would be purchased by the Police Federation and original sponsoring clubs.

The Council voted unanimously to name the park after Anoka Police Dog King and to construct the base for the statue. All of the council members were well aware of the exploits of King and the fact that he regularly visited elementary schools and was considered a friend and protector. They all believed it was simply good community relations to name this park for this famous police dog and place a statue of him in the park.

On May 7, 1977, during National Police Week the new park dedicated to police dog King was to be dedicated. The master of ceremonies at the dedication of King Memorial Park was Captain Ed LaTuff. Captain LaTuff commanded the Administrative and Investigative Arm of the Police Department. The Mayor at the time of this dedication was Charlie Sell. He along with the former Mayor Don Scarborough unveiled the statue of King. Mr. Scarborough was mayor when the park naming was approved. A bronze plaque on the front of the brick base read, "King Memorial Park- In Memory of Anoka's first police dog. He was a friend and protector of all Anokan's. Sponsored by Anoka Police Federation, Anoka Lions Club, Anoka Jaycees, Anoka American Legion Post 102. A life size concrete statue of a German shepherd, painted to look like King was placed atop a five foot brick base. Don Melrose, who was a councilmember and a teacher from Sandburg Middle School had members of his class read essays on the value of dogs. The main speaker at this event was Anoka County Undersheriff Don Dwyer. Mr. Dwyer was a former Minneapolis Police Chief. He spoke very highly about the value of police dogs.

Minnesota Governor Al Quie signs a proclamation proclaiming the week of August 3, 1979 to be Police Dog Week in Minnesota. With the Governor are Anoka Police Captain Andrew C. Revering, Chief Judge of the U.S. Police Canine Association Regional Police Dog Trials, St. Paul Officer Jim Cocchiarella, National Trials Chairman, Anoka Police Dog Tobey, and his handler, Officer Mike Schoephoerster.

At the end of all the ceremonies I addressed the crowd present and narrated a police dog demonstration. We had police dogs taking part in the demonstration from the Cities of Anoka, Coon Rapids, and Blaine Police Departments. It should be noted that on May 20, 1988 during National Police Week the concrete statue of King was replaced with a life size bronze statue. The concrete statue had over the years had become worn and damaged. The bronze statue was developed by famous Minneapolis bronze artist Roger Brodin. He constructed the statue by using photographs of King. The statue was paid for by the Anoka Police Federation.

In April 1994, Cable TV star Rin Tin Tin K9 Cop, visited
Anoka to promote the DARE program. He is shown
here with Chief Andy Revering at the bronze statue of
Anoka Police dog King in King Memorial Park.

I went on to eventually become the police chief in the City of
Anoka. I continued to be involved with police dog work as a Judge
and sometimes Host in Regional and National Police Dog Trials. I
always took the opportunity to speak at police dog demonstrations
and tell people about King and the value of these great dogs. After
working a total of 33 years with the police department, the last 14
years as the police chief I retired in 1998. I always made sure we had
a couple of police dogs on the department while I was chief and today
police dogs are a big part of police departments across the United
States. King is given his share of the credit for that.

On October 11, 2018, a new National Law Enforcement Museum
opened up in Washington D.C. The Museum had been raising funds
for the past twenty five years in an effort to build it with private
funding. About twenty years before it opened, the museum sent
out letters to law enforcement agencies soliciting artifacts for the
proposed new museum. I contacted them at the time and told them

about a large picture of my old police dog that hung in my office to see if they wanted it. I explained to them that this picture had a kind of indented box at the bottom with a miniature bronze of King that was the same as the life size statue of him in the park. Further, his badge and Lassie Gold Award were also depicted in this picture. They inquired as to whether they could get copies of newspaper clippings of the old dogs captures. I told them we would give them everything we had on him. I didn't hear back from the Museum until a few years before the Museum was about to open. I was advised the artifacts of my old police dog were going to be displayed in the museum and was advised further that they thought I'd be pleased with what they had done. I was looking forward to the grand opening.

On October 19, 2018 The National Law Enforcement Museum in a newsletter, named King and I among twenty five U.S. Law Enforcement Pioneers. It was a humbling honor. We were listed with such notables as August Vollmer, the Father of Modern Law Enforcement, Sir Thomas Dale, the first Lawman in the Colonies, J. Edgar Hoover, The FBI's first Director, former President Theodore Roosevelt, who was once a Commissioner of the New York Police Department, Allan Pinkerton, the President's Detectives, Bass Reeves, Frontier Lawman Extraordinaire, and Frank Serpico, just to name a few. I did take note that this was primarily an old person's club, as Serpico and I were the only ones still alive.

The museum had set several dates that they had planned to open, but because of a shortage in fund raising it kept getting delayed. Finally, the building was completed and firm Grand Opening date was set for October 11th, 2018.

I went out to attend the grand opening of the new National Law Enforcement Museum with my son, Eric, my daughter Stephanie and her husband Steve Voss, my good friend and former Sheriff of Anoka County Ken Wilkinson and his wife Patricia and their son Steve, and my good friend Jay Julian and his wife Terry. At the grand opening ceremony the first speaker was Clint Eastwood, the famous Hollywood movie actor, producer, and director. Mr. Eastwood is Honorary Chairman of the National Law Enforcement Museum. Many other notable speakers also took part in the ceremonies, and in a reception line after the speeches I got a chance to meet Mr. Eastwood. I gave him a commemorative coin with King's picture on it and told him, "Mr. Eastwood, that's my dog." He said, "If that's your dog, I'll be keeping the coin, "and he put it in his pocket. After the ceremonies we went inside to view the Museum.

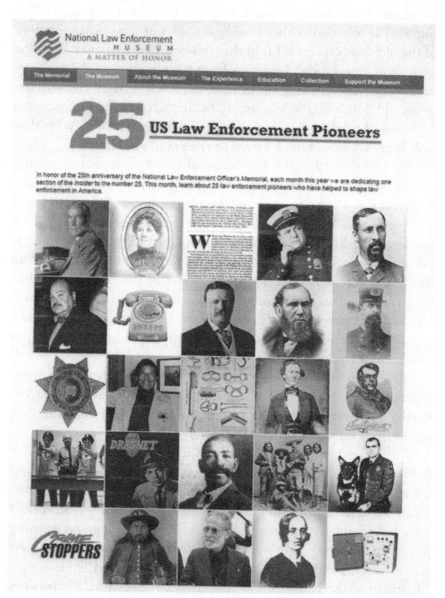

The new museum was built to be primarily underground with glass ground level entrances. As we entered the museum and began to walk down the stairway to the main underground level, my daughter said, "Dad look up there on the wall."

Chief Andy Revering, police dog King's former handler speaks to local Washington D.C. reporter. Image of King and Chief Revering projected on huge wall in museum.

When I looked where she was pointing, there were several very large pictures projected on the upper level wall of law enforcement related events. In among those pictures was a picture of King and me. Once again, it was a terribly humbling and proud moment, which brought a tear to my eye seeing my old dog up there. As we walked down into the museum we observed a very professional group of displays depicting the different aspects of the law enforcement field. We finally entered an area that appeared to be related strictly to police dogs, and there on a table was a boxed in display with a glass top depicting the artifacts related to King's service. Inside the display was an old black and white photograph of King and I and the dates we served. It was the same photograph that was being projected on that large wall. Also displayed was a miniature of the same bronze life size statue of King displayed in the park named in his honor. His badge was also there along with his Lassie Gold Award for Meritorious Service, presented to him by the producers of the Lassie Television Show, for capturing an armed gunman who had shot to people. A copy of a coloring book with King on the cover was in the display. The coloring books are passed out on a regular basis by the police department to school children. The most unique thing probably in the display is a beer can with King's picture on the front.

Display case of King at the National Law Enforcement Museum.

As a fundraiser for the Anoka County Humane Society one year, the local liquor store was given permission to use King's photo on specially produced beer cans. I'm told it was a successful campaign. Finally, there is a plaque in this display which tells the observer who King is.

I always had fond memories of that old dog. He was truly the best partner I ever worked with. For him and I to be honored at a National level in this fashion truly leaves me without words. I will never forget him.

Chapter 12

POLICE DOGS AS REASONABLE FORCE

The final chapter of this book is taken from an article co-written by Chief Judge Emeritus James T. Knutson of the Anoka County District and County Courts in Anoka, Minnesota and myself which appeared as the cover story in the Minnesota Police Chief Magazine in the summer of 1983. The argument presented is important as it was the same as I made in 1967 for the lawful and effective use of police dogs as non-lethal force and is still an effective argument today.

Is the use of police dogs in making apprehensions of suspects a reasonable and justifiable use of force? The answer to this question cannot be sought by a simple yes or no without examining the total ramifications of the use of force in general.

USE OF FORCE IN GENERAL

Generally stated, the duty of an officer to make an arrest necessarily carries with it the right to employ such reasonable degree of force as may be necessary to take the offender into custody. On the other hand, the use of force which is excessive or un-necessary depending on the particular circumstances of the case, is unjustified and may subject the officer to criminal as well as civil liability.[1]

There is some distinction between the amount of force which may be used in making an arrest for a felony and for a misdemeanor.[2]

In making an arrest in performance of his duty, the officer enjoys a special protection afforded him/her by the law. As stated by the Supreme Court of Iowa:[3]

An officer, in the performance of his duty as such, stands on an entirely different footing from an individual. He is a minister of justice, and entitled to the peculiar protection of the law. Without submission to his authority there is no security, and anarchy reigns supreme. He must, of necessity, be the aggressor, and the law affords him/her special protection. In his capacity as an individual he may take advantage of the "first law of nature," and defend himself against assault; as an officer he has an affirmative duty to perform, and in the performance therefore he should, so long as he keeps within due bounds, be protected. Sentimentalism should not go as far as to obstruct the due administration of law, and brute force should not be permitted to obstruct the wheels of justice.

Such protection, however, is conferred only when the officer is proceeding in a lawful manner; and unless he has authority to make the particular arrest, any force used by him/her is unjustified. The law cloaks him with this protection only while he is making a lawful arrest.

Authority to use reasonable force in effecting an arrest is commonly provided by statute, usually declaratory of the common law in this respect.[4]

Traditionally, a suspect submits to custody. However, we find a growing element that does not respect tradition or the physical presence of a police officer. Resisting arrest, often with the aid from police-hating allies, is becoming quite common. In 1960, 9.621 peace officers were assaulted in this country, whereas in 1980, 57,847 peace officers were assaulted.

Contrast this rise in assaults on officers with the ease with which a police officer, along with a trained dog, has often been able to control a mob. In these successes, there is no outnumbered police officer who must wait for the development of exact situations before he dares to draw his gun for so much as a threat. There is not indecision to encourage the pack, only the certainty in the way his alerted dog squares off to meet the first aggressive move.[5]

REASONABLE FORCE

The law is not disposed to hold peace officers to any strict, precise measurement of the degree of force necessary under a given state of facts. As stated by one federal court, the courts should not "lay down rules which will make it so dangerous for officers to perform their duties that they will shrink and hesitate from action which the proper protection of society demands. "Thus, the determining factor is not whether the force used was somewhat in excess of what may be regarded as absolutely necessary in light of subsequent calm deliberation, but whether it was grossly out of proportion to the emergency as it appeared to the officer at the time. As stated in a Missouri case.[6]

An officer in making an arrest should use no unnecessary violence: but, it being his duty to make the arrest, the law clothes him/her with the power to accomplish that result. His duty is to overcome all resistance, and bring the party to be arrested under physical restraint; and the means he may use must be co-extensive with the duty, and so the law is written.

The degree of force permitted an officer in making an arrest depends upon the circumstances of the particular case and may not in any case be disproportionate to the resistance offered. As stated by the Supreme Court of New Jersey:[7]

The force used may not be more than what reasonably appears to be necessary.....Whether the force used exceeded the needs of the occasion is to be determined on the basis of the facts as they reasonably appeared to the officer at the time of the occurrence.

POLICE DOGS

Whether the force used was excessive is a question of fact to be determined in the light of all circumstances of each particular case, judged by the standards of an ordinary prudent person in the position of the officer at the time. Statutes establishing the permissible force to be used in making arrests are found in many states.[8]

A considerable amount of discretion is permitted the officer in gauging the amount of force reasonably necessary to effect an arrest. As stated by the West Virginia Supreme Court of Appeals:[9]

An officer in making an arrest is presumed to act in good faith as to the extent of the force employed by him/her. He/she must not employ force carelessly or unnecessarily. If he/she does so and injures the accused, he will be penalized. This is a jury question. But the officer is primarily the judge of the extent of the force to be employed by him under the circumstances, and he will not be deemed to have exercised excessive force unless it appears he/she has abused his/her power and authority. His/her conduct in such circumstances will not be weighed in gold scales....In the stress of such circumstances. If an officer uses greater force than circumstances really require, as later deliberately appraised by a court or jury in the tranquility of a courtroom, such appraisal does not necessarily operate in condemnation of the officer. His conduct must be weighed in the light of circumstances as they arose.

But the officer is not the final, arbitrary judge as to this question, it is ultimately a matter for the court or jury to decide. In such determination the officer is aided by the presumptions that he acted in good faith and in the proper performance of his duty.[10]

The courts have held, when reasonably necessity exists, that it is permissible for a peace officer to use a baton, mace, or similar weapon in order to subdue a prisoner or overcome his resistance to arrest.

For the past one hundred years, it has been the custom of sheriff's, police, constables, and other officials entrusted with enforcement of the law to use dogs in tracking down and apprehending felons, burglars, murderers, and other law violators.

Actions of the dogs, where it is shown that they are well trained, have been received and accepted by the courts in Oklahoma, Alabama, Kentucky, Missouri, Texas, Arkansas, Tennessee, Louisiana, North Carolina, Florida, and Georgia.

In Great Britain, the use of dogs was sought several years ago to assist the unarmed English Bobbie in tracking down and apprehending thugs and burglars. The British example in the use of police dogs as a non-lethal police tool to aid in apprehensions of suspects has set a pattern which is being followed throughout the world.

Canadians have been using police dogs since the 1930s. In a recent Canadian homicide, a police service dog of the Royal Canadian Mounted Police picked up a scent at the crime scene and tracked down the killer. The scenting ability of the police dog in this case was the main cause for a circumstantial evidence conviction.[11]

Police dogs are not considered to be deadly force by the law enforcement authorities who engage their use, and this fact is generally spelled out quite clearly in operational guidelines and policies. The dogs are trained to take a "controlled bite" or a single engagement of a suspect, and to hang on until the resistance is ceased or a signal is given to cease engagement. The injury sustained is very minimal, unless the suspect fights the dog.

While authorities frequently call attention to a distinction between the degree of force permissible in making an arrest for a felony and one for a misdemeanor, according to the weight of authority, there is little, if any difference in this respect insofar as effecting the arrest is concerned when forcible resistance is offered. Under the general rule, if a misdemeanant resists arrest, the officer may employ such force as may be reasonably necessary to overcome such resistance and subject the offender to his custody. When arresting a person charged only with a misdemeanor, an officer is not compelled to retreat upon meeting resistance, however violent; and provided he acts in good faith and not maliciously, he may be justified in the use of deadly force to accomplish the arrest. This is true, however, only when the offender is actually resisting to such an extent as to place the officer in danger of great bodily injury or death, particularly when the party is defying the officer with a deadly weapon.

Obviously, if the law is to be enforced, the officer cannot be required to desist and retire in the face of opposition. It is his duty to press forward and subdue the assailant. He may meet force with like force when reasonably necessary, and this means he may be justified in taking the life of the offender when this becomes necessary in order to protect himself and complete the arrest.[12]

AS EXPRESSED BY THE KENTUCKY
COURT OF APPEALS:[13]

Manifestly an officer has no right to wantonly shoot or kill one only charged with a misdemeanor if the offender is merely trying to escape such arrest by flight; but if the offender be armed and offers forcible resistance or threatens the officer, and, in connection with such threat, assumes a menacing attitude towards the officer, the officer then may use such force in the exercise of a sound judgment as is necessary to effect the arrest, not only for the purpose of bringing the offender to justice, but to protect himself from threatened danger.

ON THE SAME POINT, THE SUPREME
COURT OF MISSISSIPPI ELABORATED:[14]

An officer may, of course, resort to the use of firearms to subdue a misdemeanant whom he is attempting to arrest if it is reasonably apparent to the officer that by reason of disparity in size and strength between him/her and the misdemeanant, and this even though the misdemeanant may be wholly unarmed.

Pointing out that the officer necessarily must be the aggressor in the undertaking to arrest a misdemeanant and is not denied the right of self-defense merely because he is the aggressor, the court continued:[15]

He is still, however, not justified in resorting to the use of firearms to repel the attack of an unarmed misdemeanant not his superior in physical strength and power, since such attack does not furnish reasonable grounds to anticipate danger to life or great bodily harm.

The same principles have been held applicable in cases where a third party forcibly assaults the officer in attempting to rescue a misdemeanant from his custody.[16]

While generally repudiating the theory that use of deadly force in making an arrest is limited to felony cases or self-defense, practically all courts hold an officer has no right to employ deadly force on or against a misdemeanant who offers no resistance but is merely attempting to escape, running away, or failing to obey the officer's commands to halt, even though he cannot be taken otherwise. This is the chief distinction between the use of deadly force in arrest for felony and for misdemeanor. The reason given for the difference was succinctly stated in an Iowa case shortly following the turn of the century.[17]

In such cases it is better, and more in consonance with modern notions regarding the sanctity of human life, that the offender escape than that his life be taken, in a case where the extreme penalty would be a trifling fine or a few days imprisonment in jail.

A few moments of thought will show anyone why the speed of a dog can be a tremendous factor, physically and psychologically, in those instances where a suspect must be apprehended while on foot and without the use of deadly force. In addition to the obvious advantages of on-the-scene apprehension, there is another factor in these times of fast cars and crowded streets. Chases that dogs can resolve while the suspects are still on foot often develop into mechanized nightmares when the suspect reaches his or someone else's car ahead of pursuit. Certainly a means of taking a suspect on foot whenever possible is more necessary today than it was when cars were less available.[18]

The justification for the distinction in apprehension traces back to the ancient common law concept of misdemeanor as a strictly minor offense whereas all crimes of any consequence were felonies.

AS STATED BY THE SUPREME COURT OF NORTH CAROLINA:[19]

It was thought that to permit the life of one charged with a mere misdemeanor to be taken, when not resisting but only fleeing, would, aside from its inhumanity, be productive of more evil than good. The reason for the distinction was obvious. Ordinarily, the security of a person and property is not endangered by a misdemeanant being at large, while the safety and security of society require the speedy arrest and punishment of a felon.

POLICE DOGS AS REASONABLE FORCE:

As stated previously, use of police dogs is not considered use of deadly force, when such dogs are highly trained to apprehend and hold. They should be employed as not only an alternative to deadly force in felonious situations, but also as a replacement for deadly force in apprehending fleeing misdemeanants.

Some authorities broadly declare the rule to be that an officer has no right to use deadly force in making an arrest of one charged only with a misdemeanor, either in effecting the arrest or stopping the flight of the offender. Except in self-defense. Others seek to justify use of extreme force in such cases as involving the right of self-defense against such violent resistance as threatens the officer's personal safety. But practically all of the cases cited as authority for these overstatements of the law involved situations in which an officer had shot or wounded an escaping misdemeanant or one fleeing from arrest, instances in which the right is generally denied in any event.[20]

It seems apparent that a police dog trained in the art of apprehending a fleeing suspect is the medium which could be used to satisfy the argument on both sides.

An officer attempting to make a lawful arrest in any case may defend himself by using reasonable force for his own protection when necessary, although he may not use excessive force in retaliation. The mere fact that an unresisting offender uses abusive language toward him does not justify the use of force on that account alone. Neither is an officer entitled to the full right of self-defense while he/she is acting illegally.[21]

It must be remembered that police dogs only perform in a manner for which they have been trained. Generally, they respond only on command or react on their own if their handler is being attacked. It is therefore important to recognize that the dog will not normally make a mistake. The human officer must be the one held accountable for errors in the use of the dog as force. The dog cannot perceive justified or unjustified force, it only reacts to training and commands.

The right of an arresting officer to use deadly force to overcome violent resistance by a misdemeanant is sometimes justified by the courts on the grounds of self-defense; the right of an officer to defend himself against assault and his right to use aggressive force to effect the arrest are by no means the same thing.[22]

Occasionally it has been said that an officer is excused from responsibility for killing a misdemeanant solely on the ground of self-defense, and no doubt there is a close relation between the rights of an officer who finds himself resisted by a criminal and the rights of a private individual upon whom a dangerous attack is made by another. But text writers and courts are generally agreed that the force which an officer may exert differs from the resistance that may be offered in self-defense. The officer making the arrest may; of course, defend himself, as may any other person who is assaulted, but the law does not stop here. The officer must of necessity be the aggressor; his mission is not accomplished when he wards off the assault; he must press forward and accomplish his objective; he is not bound to put off the arrest until a more favorable time. Because of these duties devolved upon him, the law throws around him a special protection.

ON THIS POINT, THE OBSERVATIONS OF A NOTED TEXT WRITER ARE PERTINENT.[23]

Defensive force must be distinguished from force employed solely for the purpose of apprehension. The arrester, if placed in danger, by the violence of the arrestee, may use whatever force reasonably seems necessary to save himself from death or great bodily harm—and he may do this without abandoning the effort to arrest, and whether the arrest is for felony or misdemeanor…Hence he may "freely and without retreating repel force by force."

The point that serves most strongly to buttress these principles is that the duty of the officer to be the aggressor and press forward to place the person under restraint is not accomplished by purely defensive action on his part or by requiring him to retreat upon encountering resistance . Otherwise, the law would be encouraging resistance to deter forthright action by officers attempting to arrest misdemeanants. To require an officer to desist from his efforts to arrest merely because an offender displays violent unwillingness to submit would be a boon to the riotous and lawless element, to the detriment of public peace and tranquility.[24]

A question often asked is, "why haven't more cities acknowledged the proven value of dogs?' There are two possible answers to this question: First, a completely illogical prejudice against police dogs: second, hesitancy on the part of police officials who claim that the guns their officers carry are less offensive to the minority groups than dogs would be.

In Los Angeles, in 1965, where the use of dogs had been strongly rejected, and the point of not offending an individual's dignity had been honored to the ultimate degree. During the city's Watts riots, in at least several instances where dogs could have changed the course of action, gunfire provided some individuals with a guarantee that their dignity would be permanently protected against offenses. They're dead. Since that time the LAPD has developed a highly successful police dog program.[25]

USE OF EXCESSIVE FORCE

If an officer uses more force than is reasonably necessary under the circumstances in making an arrest, whether for felony or misdemeanor, he thereby renders himself civilly as well as criminally liable, just the same as any private individual under the same circumstances. Police officers have no right to act oppressively or to injure their prisoners wantonly or unnecessarily unlawful conduct on the part of the officer deprives him of the protection which the law otherwise would afford him, rendering him a trespasser.[26]

It has been held that an officer who exceeds the amount of force is privileged to use under the circumstances is liable for only so much of the force as is excessive. Also, it has been held that a peace officer is liable for the use of excessive force only when he acts maliciously or in wanton abuse of his authority.[27]

Liability for such conduct may follow when an innocent bystander is injured or killed, or when the officer is attempting to arrest the wrong person.[28]

While the use of unnecessary or excessive force by an officer making an otherwise lawful arrest may subject him to civil or criminal liability, this does not affect the validity of the arrest.[29]

Ultimate determination of the reasonableness and necessity for the degree of force used by the officer is for the court or jury. The burden of proving excessive force is upon the party asserting it.[30]

District Judge Leon York of Payne County, Oklahoma, stated upon hearing a case before him:[31]

There are many well- meaning and sensitive people who join in the hue and cry of brutality and thus accuse the police. But I ask, who is the real culprit? The vendor of illegal drugs and noxious weeds who seeks to profit at the expense and misery of his victims, our young people, or the police who are trying to do their job? What does it mean if there are a few slashed wrists or torn clothes? It may be that

Sir Walter Scott was right when he wrote, and men have said that the finger of God was in it. Dogs strike terror in the hearts of the guilty and the wicked, and I dare say that if all police departments throughout our country were equipped with police dogs, hard drugs and marijuana would disappear from the American scene.

I rule in favor of the dog.

POLICE DOGS ARE NOT DEADLY FORCE

The U.S. 9th Circuit Court in San Francisco ruled that Unleashing a police dog on a fleeing suspect is not deadly force because police dogs are not likely to kill suspects.

In summary, police dogs are a legitimate, non-lethal police tool which may be employed when force must be used making apprehensions of resisting suspects. Dogs should be considered and deployed as an alternative to deadly force when dealing with felonious offenders and as an absolute replacement for deadly force in controlling resisting or fleeing misdemeanants.

FOOTNOTES

1. Edward C. Fischer, Laws of Arrest. Ed. Robert I. Donigan (Illinois. The Traffic Institute, Northwestern University, 1967) 295.
2. Ibid.
3. Ibid. pp. 294-295
4. Ibid p. 296
5. William R. Koehler, The Koehler Method of Guard Dog Training(New York. Howell Book House Inc. 1967) p. 76
6. Fischer, p. 296
7. Ibid. p. 297
8. Ibid. p. 297
9. Ibid. pp 297-298
10. Ibid. p 298
11. Ibid. p. 299
12. Ibid. pp. 301-302
13. Ibid. p. 302
14. Ibid. pp. 303-303
15. Ibid. p. 303
16. Ibid. p. 303
17. Ibid. p. 304
18. Koehler. P. 75
19. Fischer. P. 304
20. Ibid. pp. 304-305
21. Ibid. p. 305
22. Ibid. p. 305
23. Ibid. pp. 305-306
24. Ibid. p. 306
25. Koehler. Pp. 71-72
26. Fischer. P. 306

27. Ibid. p. 306

28. Ibid. p. 306

29. Ibid. pp. 306-307

30. Ibid. p. 307

31. Leon J. York, The Dog as a Legal Witness (National Police Journal: Autumn. 1973). P. 8

ABOUT THE AUTHORS

James T. Knutson was the Chief Judge Of the District and County Courts of Anoka, Minnesota. Judge Knutson Received his J.D. degree from the University of Minnesota in 1949, and began his law practice in Ortonville, Minnesota, prior to moving to Anoka In 1951. He was appointed Municipal Judge in 1951 and County Judge in Probate court in 1967. He was Chief Judge until his retirement.

Andrew C. Revering was the Chief of Police in the City of Anoka for 14 years. He served on the police department for 33 years. Mr. Revering served as a patrolman, police dog handler, detective, sergeant, captain, and Chief. Mr. Revering holds an AA Degree from North Hennepin Community College, a BA Degree from St. Cloud State University, and is a graduate of the FBI National Academy 101st Session. Prior to serving on the police department he served as a U.S.A.F. Air Police Sentry Dog Handler for four years.

Made in the USA
Columbia, SC
20 November 2023

26534437R00078